ENGAGED

ENGAGED

When Love Takes Roots

William L. Coleman

Tyndale House
Publishers, Inc.
Wheaton, Illinois

ACKNOWLEDGMENTS

*Many friends have helped by spending
hours reading this manuscript. My special
thanks go to Mark and Doreen Olson,
Cliff Jensen, Zandee Nelson, and Clint and
Cindy Petersen.
I also want to thank Lois Janzen for
typing the book.*

UNLESS OTHERWISE NOTED,
SCRIPTURE QUOTATIONS ARE FROM
THE LIVING BIBLE.

Dedicated to
SPENCER BOONE
ERV NASE
DAVID HAMBURG
CHARLES BRUYNELL
TOM LEADER

CONTENTS

Better Together!
9

ONE
You Control Love
11

TWO
The Engagement Elevator
20

THREE
*Good People Make
Good Marriages*
28

FOUR
Changing Relationships
37

FIVE
*The Fun of
Marrying a Stranger*
45

SIX
A Great Marriage
54

SEVEN
The "Hidden" Problem
60

EIGHT
Sexual Limbo
69

NINE
Love Communicates
76

TEN
Getting Good Advice
84

ELEVEN
Haunted Houses
92

TWELVE
Mixed Couples
99

THIRTEEN
Do You Want Children?
106

FOURTEEN
You Can Never Go Home
115

FIFTEEN
Married Sex Is Fun
125

SIXTEEN
Quick Tips
137

SEVENTEEN
Weddings and Honeymoons
142

EIGHTEEN
Future Family—A.D. 2000
148

BETTER TOGETHER!

It's good to know some things never change. Couples are still holding hands and saying silly things. They walk in parks, buy crazy gifts, and see magic in rainbows. Love laughs at jokes no one else would think funny. Love can talk for an hour and never say anything.

Love is hope. Love says there will be a bright tomorrow because we have each other.

Eventually love looks for its peak in marriage. Maybe that's where you are looking now. This book is aimed at helping you sort through and give marriage the fantastic start it deserves.

As you read I hope you will be able to gain good tools for the happy years ahead. Possibly you will be able to throw off a fear here or a myth there.

Above all else, I hope you can come a little closer to seeing how great God wants marriage to be.

With your eyes wide open, enter into one of the greatest experiences you can ever know. I think you will find life better together than any other way.

William L. Coleman
Aurora, Nebraska

1

YOU CONTROL LOVE

Love is one of the most enjoyable mysteries in life. It can carry us higher than we ever expected to go. Love can also be a whirlpool of uncertainty and frustration. Yet, for all its extremes, most of us wouldn't miss it for anything.

The majority of us will follow love until it eventually leads to a marriage altar, complete with candles and freshly cut flowers. Before we step over this threshold into a new life, we need to ask some helpful questions. How much of love is merely a passing emotion? How much is a fad? Are we really caught up in something we have not even begun to understand? What role does God play in the scenario? Is love even important to a marriage?

If there are times when we feel confused about love, we shouldn't think we are alone. The author of Proverbs said there were four things he couldn't understand. You guessed number four! He couldn't figure out the growth of love between a man and a woman (30:19).

I can still see Stan and Sue sitting in my office. They were grappling with the same taffy most of us have pulled. The more they stretched to understand their love, the stickier it got. Their problem seemed simple, almost ridiculous. They loved each other greatly. They were bright college students with excellent futures. Nothing seemed to stand between them and a thoroughly happy marriage—nothing except their own fears and confusion. They needed someone to talk to to help them get a clear view of love.

The hundreds of thousands of Stans and Sues don't need a scientific dissection of love. Sometimes we become so academic we tear the tenderness out of simple passion. Love is more an art than a science. The fact is you can't have 3.2 children. No family has 3.7 members. One third of your engagement can't break up. You are a person and not an average.

There are some things which can be said with pinpoint accuracy. However, love is dynamic. It pulsates, it changes. Thank God, some days it's blind, deaf, and speechless. None of this should change. Three cheers for moonlight and roses. Long live walks in the park and a tender touch. Who can ever forget a pair of eyes that once turned your knees to jello?

But inside we all know this is only part of the picture. In order for love to last, it has to be more than a sunny feeling.

There are certain facts which must be rehearsed about love. Otherwise they are forgotten or distorted. How could anyone foul up something as basic to life as love? Through movies, books, divorces, greed, and unfaithfulness we seem to manage. Fortunately, the Bible offers us guidelines to get us back on course.

A young lady said, "I don't like what Tom says and I don't like what he does. Even my friends don't care for him. But I can't help it, I'm in love with him."

She represents what is probably the most misunderstood fact about love. Too many of us still think love is something we can never control. This simple mistake may do more damage than any other.

The fact is that love is stronger and more vital because we can partially control it. It is also the greatest guarantee that our marriage will last.

Track down love in the New Testament. The Bible commands me to love my wife, my neighbor, my enemies, and even God himself. How terribly unfair if I can't control love. I answer back, "But I don't feel a love for my wife. It isn't my fault." God's law still doesn't change. He tells me to love my wife. He knows I can control how I feel.

Many of us have been completely misled by the phrase "falling in love." It sounds like a sudden infection. Love either hits you or it doesn't. When it does, you can't do anything about it. If love misses you, your situation is just as hopeless. Many of us sit around waiting to see if the "love bug" will bite.

Life often seems simpler if we can blame everything on another force. That's why Satan gets accused of so much. God also gets blamed for many things he didn't start. The same desire to escape responsibility has kept a chubby little fellow in a diaper alive— Cupid is stupid. The responsibility for love and its fantastic benefits rests squarely on our own shoulders.

Years ago, booklets which helped us with our love life were popular. Titles promising magic formulas sold like heartburn tablets. We wanted someone else to make our decisions. Maybe a referee to call us "out" or "safe."

The greater maturity is to accept the decision as ours. In the final analysis I must determine if I choose to be in love. Then I know no trick of fate has trapped me. I love because I choose to love. We hold our heart in our own hands. No one can steal it. When I find someone I want, I will give it to him with enthusiasm.

Ann was enormously in love. Her face sang. She had a sparkle like the diamond she wore.

"I don't know what it is," she said, "but when I look into his eyes there is something that melts me."

What does she see? Why don't her girl friends see the same thing? The only magic in his eyes is what Ann puts there. She sees something special because she chooses to love him.

This principle becomes more important with each passing year. After you have been married fifteen years you might ask yourself, "Why do we stay together?" There may be younger people you find more attractive. Many of your friends may be divorced.

Why do you stay together? Because you choose to love each other. It is a conscious and voluntary decision. It is not based on a feeling which may shift with the next wind. It is based on a feeling you choose to stimulate.

Many young people protest. They insist love is not so easy to handle. You can't just turn it on and off like the knobs on a television. Of course, they are correct. No passion is easy to control. But passion should not be allowed to run wild. We must not be angry without restraint. We cannot be joyful without boundaries. We dare not love without control.

It isn't easy to be the master over love. But it is essential. It is sane. It is filled with beautiful hope.

Could we love someone else? Certainly! Most of us have and could again. By selecting one person to love we have drawn our boundaries. We will love no one else in the same way we choose to love this person.

Mature love is more than just feeling. I see someone walking at a shopping mall and I say to myself, I could love her. That is merely a feeling. I don't know her, her personality, her values, her tolerance. It is a gut-level feeling.

Lasting love is a passion which grows. The more we know the person, the more deeply we love him.

There are a few who are struck like lightning. The minute they see somone they hear violins. This usually happens only in the movies. As one writer has suggested, it *has* to be "love at first sight" in a show that only has two hours to run.

Surveys continuously support love by growth. The overwhelming majority say they did not "fall in love" all at once. They met a person and found him attractive or interesting. Whatever caught their attention made them want to learn more. Possibly they met the person again or went on a date. At any rate, something started to grow. The person became more interesting.

Some people are frustrated because falling in love wasn't like a divine revelation or a heart seizure. Consequently they even wonder if it is real. Such "falling" is a romantic dream that most of us have never experienced. But love which takes time can be the most enduring kind.

On the opposite side of the ledger, many instant romances have enormous difficulties. Dr. Paul Landis studied people who met and married within six weeks. Four out of five ended in divorce. There is much to be said for the time and growth approach.

It is a question of expectation. Those who expect love to be automatic and instantaneous are often disappointed. It is more realistic to expect love to grow into full bloom as you live together in marriage. Then, rather than looking for an ideal experience, both lovers expect to change and grow.

A couple who have been married for twenty years say, "We are more in love today than we were when we got married." It may sound like a polite bluff, but it also may be the exact truth. Experiences both of cohesion and adversity have caused their love to mature.

Hopefully a person enters a marriage with a flexible attitude. He is not afraid of change. One year from now he will be a different person. Ideally he can hardly wait to see what the improvements are

One of the most beautiful love stories in the Bible is about Isaac and Rebekah. They had never met each other. Their marriage was arranged by Isaac's father and servant. Yet their romance is gorgeous partly because their expectations were high. Never having met, they had already decided to love each other.

"And Isaac brought Rebekah into his mother's tent, and she became his wife. He loved her very much, and she was a special comfort to him after the loss of his mother" (Gen. 24:67).

Contrary to popular belief, the first-century attitude toward divorce among Jews was wide open. A man could dismiss his wife for practically no cause. And yet, divorce was rare. A Jewish author said the reason for so few divorces was simple: they didn't want to get divorced.

It is again a question of expectation. One couple has decided to try marriage and see if it works out. Another couple sees it as utopia. The realistic person sees it as a magnificent opportunity to grow in love and change.

Since love is so subjective, it is easy to fool ourselves. Many marry for strange motives. One lady in ill health married a man for financial security; her husband wasn't wealthy, but he had an income. A high school graduate married so she would not have to face the working world. Her goal was to have a child and become a housewife as quickly as possible. Both of them lived to wish they were single. Yet each had told herself she was in love.

Many marry a good body and call it love. One man said, "I was determined to marry the best body in the county. Two weeks after the wedding the thrill wore off and we realized we had nothing in common." Today they are divorced.

There are too many heading for an altar who do not really love each other. The pressures of life have pushed them together, and their lack of commitment may eventually catch up with them and completely gut their relationship.

Peg and Ron once had an exhilarating love. They were in their late teens and had gone together for two years. The first year of their engagement was immature but beautiful. Then the relationship started falling apart as their interests changed.

Peg's mother disliked Ron like taxes. (Actually, she hated him but couldn't use the word.) Mother was outspoken and tried hard to break them up. The second year they stayed engaged because they refused to let Mom win. Their love was gone, but they were welded together by a mutual enemy. They were determined to withstand her. Fortunately, they had enough sense not to marry. Unfortunately, some couples *are* marrying because of mutual problems rather than mutual love.

Even love is not enough reason to get married. If I love a green Cadillac, that is no reason to buy one. I cannot afford the payments. My garage is too small. The car burns gas too greedily. And yet I lust for it greatly. I would love to have it. But it is a marriage which will never work.

Many of us have met someone it would be easy to love. The person's attractiveness and personality are tremendous. However, we realize that his goals, interests, and idiosyncrasies would explode against ours. We decide to redirect our love. But some of it would have been nice—it really would have been.

There are several people you could love—more than one you could be extremely happy with. It would be thrilling to think there might be a "one and only"; a knight in shining armor who would one day appear on a hill. It only happens in commercials.

Love is a compromise. You will know you are mature enough to love when you are ready to give and take.

How do I know if I am in love? It's a frequent question in a highly romanticized society. The easiest answer has been an evasive, "When the time comes, you will know." There is some truth to this old saw.

Probably a more accurate reply is, "When you find a person you could love, you will know it." True love is too personal to lend itself to magic formulas. Find a person to whom you can give yourself—whether you are a man or a woman—and you have found someone you can love.

Too often we suffer by making too many comparisons. We want a love life just like our sister or brother has. We hope for a romance similar to the couple in our neighborhood. Worst of all, we look for a movie-star romance.

We are individuals. Our love life will be like no one else's. It will not necessarily be better, but it will definitely be different.

Most of us have learned that love is no cure-all. The problems affecting marriage are obvious all around us. Thousands of marriages are dropping faster than the dollar.

We need to write this axiom where we can read it daily: "Love and marriage solve almost no problems." They intensify many difficulties, but they erase almost none.

Love is a joy. It will give you many things to smile about—even to laugh out loud. It must be the best tonic any of us can get without a prescription. But love has its boundaries and limitations.

A young man is unsure of himself and worries immensely. He is convinced that if only he had a loving companion he would gain confidence. After the initial novelty of marriage wears off, he reverts to the same fearful person he was.

Some problems are too deeply ingrained to be eradicated by simple love.

Before we decide to give our love to a person, we should answer this: Can I be happy with this person if he never changes? Too often we love an imaginary figure rather than the real thing. After we are married, we will get him to slim down. We know we can talk her into wearing contacts once we have settled down. We can live in the Midwest for a couple of years, but then I'll talk him into moving to the coast.

But what if he doesn't change? Can you live with that temper? Are you content to live a sedentary life? What if he doesn't change his mind about children?

Give your love to the person he is now, not to the prince you hope he will become. We all know examples of people who have changed drastically after marriage. However, don't count on it. It is possible the change may be the opposite of what you hoped.

Love is not an irresistible force. You can probably remember the summer you "fell in love." For ten great weeks someone was the apple of your eye. When he left, your heart broke. Today you have pleasant memories, but it's definitely over.

Love is a controllable force. No one *needs* to fall in love. With eyes wide open, lovers can run and jump with real enthusiasm.

Statistics indicate that those who know each other well before they get married have the most enduring relationships. They have taken time to test the soil. Is it a good place for love to grow? An engagement that is too long may have a detrimental effect. Reasonable time gives love a chance to take root and get a healthy start.

Up until this commitment, most young people have only engaged in floating love. They have loved one person for a while, and then possibly someone else. The prospect of married love becomes another matter. This love finds its anchor in commitment. The two of you agree to nurture and strengthen a love for the rest of your lives. No previous love has reached this peak.

For most of us, love is essential. We want to know someone cares. When we are up, we want a special someone to know about it. When our hopes cave in, we need somebody to help dig us out.

Love gives me a special value. A person says I am worth something. Somebody thinks I am just a little clever, maybe attractive, and certainly important. Merely having that special person makes a drastic impact on my personality.

It isn't uncommon to see many loves fizzle out. They ran strong for a short distance, but there wasn't enough to sustain them.

John and Marcia suffered from love fatigue. The only thing they had in common was that they both loved John. It isn't as novel as we might like to think. After doing this for a couple of years, Marcia was worn out. She gave and gave and gave. At first she thought she was supposed to. Marcia even believed the Bible taught her that her only role was to please John. After trying it one-sidedly, she decided to throw in the towel.

Others will establish their love on a mutual career. This may be especially true of a couple starting a business. It is also frequent among Christian ministers and missionaries. When the career becomes frayed, so does the love. It is common to find a couple in career trouble who are also in love trouble.

Probably there is no stronger cable than simple friendship to hold love together. The partners don't have to share everything. They don't need to be inseparable. He might go backpacking, while she never cares to go. She loves to bowl and he has never picked up a ball. More importantly, they just like to be with each other.

Their values, religion, and mental pursuits have something in common. Even their fears may be similar. They can talk, confide, and dream together. Who is the person you would most like to talk over coffee with? If something tremendous happens, who do you want to call? Usually you call your best friend. Fortunately, your best friend is most often the person you love.

Since we control love, we want to give it carefully. We don't hand it out for the moment. Hopefully we won't distribute it quickly for something that catches our eye. We look specifically for a potential friend and lover.

"Live joyfully with the wife whom thou lovest all the days of the life of thy vanity, which he hath given thee under the sun" (Eccl. 9:9, KJV).

The fact that you control love is the greatest guarantee your marriage has. Suppose, ten years from now, you "fall in love" with someone at the office. If you can't control love, your life will become a mess. What can you do? Will you divorce your partner for your new love? Will you see the other person on the side or pine away in your heart? No. No. No. Because you control love you will stop loving the person at the office. The decision and the power are yours.

As long as you accept your responsibility in love, no one can fracture your marriage. You will have a fantastic partnership because you are in control.

2
THE ENGAGEMENT
ELEVATOR

"Some days I really get scared."

His wedding day was coming closer. Like a train chugging through the mountains, the puffing smoke was in view.

"You ought to be scared." Charlie's reply shocked him. "This is one of the most important decisions of your life. Everybody gets shook."

Charlie summed it up pretty closely. A few people never become frightened or second guess their decision to marry. The other 90 percent of us shake in our boots sooner or later. Somewhere along the line we experience everything from absolute ecstasy to numbness to staring into space to cold feet. Most people wonder if they are really going to go through with it.

"I wonder if I'm weird." He was an engaged university student. "I have so many ups and downs about this engagement, I start to think I'm not stable."

He has a lot of company. The fact is, almost half of those who get engaged call it off before the final bell rings. Nearly one out of two swim around, grope, swallow buckets of water, and finally go under.

If you have second thoughts, you are definitely part of the majority. It isn't uncommon to have a couple wrestle over the engagement ring on the night he proposes. She will take it—she won't. But what if this happens? Shouldn't I talk to my parents one more time? I'm still thinking about what my sister said. The sentences come in colorful varieties, but they all amount to the same thing. The person is often happy, frightened, and confused—all at the same time.

The important thing to remember is that most of the time engagement is an elevator. Expect the ups and the downs. They will eventually go away. Some of the best marriages we see around us started out with months of the "willies."

It is sad to see some couples collapse merely because they don't recognize this. If the engagement doesn't run smoothly, they are sure the marriage is doomed. This is not true.

We become victims of our own idealism. We expect love to rise above the bumps of life. Often it does. Love can fly with the eagles. I have never experienced any happiness like being in love. But love also hits the pavement, bounces, and fractures.

Some couples sail into rough weather. Instead of calmly handling the problem, they are shocked by the fact they have the problem at all. They didn't expect to doubt their love. They didn't expect to want to run. Rather than accepting it as a passing, natural feeling they become obsessed with it. Consequently, they never recover. One day the engagement dies a cruel death.

Thank God for broken engagements. I can remember couples who were obviously not suited. It was evident to everyone but them. The conclusions bore it out. Their marriages became alley fights. Some great people walked into terrible marriages.

Once engaged, you don't have to stay there. But don't bail out because of the normal ups and downs. You may miss something beautiful just because you got nervous.

"I just gave up trying to figure it out," said one man. "The more I tried to understand it, the more confused I got. I finally said to myself, 'I don't understand how I feel, but I'm going through with it, just believing it will all work out.'"

His marriage survived because he knew it was normal to feel confused.

Some chapters in this book are aimed directly at the "difficulties" of marriage. Group discussions are usually geared toward this emphasis.

By the time we become "warned" about all the "problems," we are bound to get a distorted view. We look at all the hazards, the pitfalls, the dangers. No wonder we become afraid of marriage.

With all the stress on these factors, it is a wonder anyone gets married.

Many people are just thrilled with being married. They enjoy the companionship, the love, the sex, the planning together, and the children.

"I don't want to get married," said a pretty teenager. "After what I've seen of my parents, it's a lousy trip."

What a shame! They have watched broken hearts on television and heard songs of wrecked marriages. Some have watched their parents fight and read depressing novels.

Someone should stand up and scream, "Stop!" Millions of married couples are as happy as mice in a granary. They wouldn't have missed marriage for anything.

When we major on the problems, we create problems.

An engaged couple becomes confronted with a disagreement and they often imagine the world has ended. They are convinced their marriage won't work. It is a bad way to begin.

Concentrate on your dreams. Most of them will come true. Read that again. Most of them will come true.

You will spend quiet evenings alone in your own living room. There will be soft music playing on the stereo. There will be a career which will grow and develop. You will spend vacations at your favorite place. Not all of your dreams will come true, but most will. Doesn't that sound great? It would be a shame to dump those dreams because of a few misunderstandings now. Most of life will not be lived under these conditions or this strain.

> *I walk in the strength of the Lord God. I tell everyone that you alone are just and good. O God, you have helped me from my earliest childhood—and I have constantly testified to others of the wonderful things you do.* Psa. 71:16, 17

What a powerfully upbeat statement about God and life. Hold on to it. There are too many good things happening to concentrate on the setbacks.

Many engaged couples have this strength in common: they can laugh together. Even the ones who were in deep distress knew they had a sense of humor. I remember one couple on the verge of separating. Their backgrounds, careers, dreams, and even their theology seemed irreconcilable to them. But still they kidded. They teased. There was a sparkle in their eyes. In your heart you knew it would work out. Underneath their stack of problems they genuinely enjoyed each other.

If you take it all too seriously, you may lose it.

The period of engagement can be both fun and frustrating. Don't let the frustrations swamp the fun.

Sometimes the longer the engagement the more chance there is for difficulties. Young people are often asking the same question: "How long should a couple be engaged?" The answer is simple: the shorter the engagement, the better off most couples are.

But you thought people had to get to know each other. You are correct. There are statistics which demonstrate that the better two people know each other the better are their chances for a happy marriage. One hundred percent right.

However, the period of engagement is *not* the best time to get to know each other. Date each other for one, two, three, ten years if you want. But once you say, "We are going to get married," do not pass Go and do not collect $200. Take the shortest route to the altar and get married. If you are not prepared to get married for a year or more, don't get engaged. It works for some but not for most.

People have all sorts of grandiose schemes as to why they must wait before they get married. If you are not ready to get married, it is generally unwise to get engaged.

"We want to work for a while and then get married." In most cases it isn't worth it. If you are rich enough to get engaged you are rich enough to get married. Get married and then work for a while.

"I have another year at college before I get married." Great! Then take another nine months before you become engaged. Absence does not necessarily make the heart beat faster.

"I want to get married but we have to wait until my mother's health is better." That is a strong reason but the answer is the same. There is no way to guess how long your mother will be sick. Don't get engaged if you are not ready to get married.

Some will object, "My sister was engaged for two years and they have the ideal marriage." They are the exception and not the rule. Get to know each other before you are engaged. Engagement periods are unusual situations and are not best geared for getting to know each other.

I heard it again just a month ago. A newly married friend said, "Tell them to keep the engagement short. It can really be tough."

Just how long you are engaged does depend on the person. But certain guidelines are true. The shorter the engagement the better off most of us are.

A large number of engaged couples are into some form of active sex. Many are unhappy and guilt-ridden. Others are trying to justify their action but honestly find it hard. Their actions and their feelings are easy to understand. Shorter engagements could greatly alleviate this problem.

It is hard to tell whether this generation is looser sexually than any previous one. The Puritans had tremendous problems trying to control sexual activity. Despite their famous law, adultery and pregnancy out of wedlock were common. Possibly other generations were just as active, but they didn't have as much open publicity.

Let's hear it for sexual activity. But let's put it inside marriage, where it belongs. Then you can exercise your freedoms and joys to your heart's content.

There are a number of storms to expect during engagement. It is important to remember they are just that—passing storms. Engagement is the season for them. After they have moved through, life will go on. Often we are better off for the experience.

One of them we can call a dust storm. It covers everything and causes everyone to choke. Dust from the parched earth can even creep through closed windows.

Engaged couples often smother and choke each other. It is natural to want to be together. Pity if you don't. You think, even dream, about each other. Most couples hang around each other constantly. Don't be surprised if sooner or later you get tired of the constant companionship. You are still in love; you have merely begun to smother.

Maybe you would like to go shopping alone. You want to go to a ball game with your other friends. If you feel that way, it doesn't mean you don't love each other. After you are married you will sometimes feel the same. Back off some. Your love can handle it. A few evenings apart may be a beautiful tonic.

By the time you adjust to the dust storm, the hailstorm will probably arrive. Hailstorms bring a million little marble-sized problems down at once. Sometimes the best example is the wedding arrangements. The strain can be terrible.

Many couples have thoroughly enjoyed their elaborate weddings. Others have come to me afterward and said, "Tell young people to elope." Different strokes for different folks.

"I ended up in the middle," said Becky. "My parents wanted a large wedding. My mom picked out the cake and the invitations.

She thought she was being so helpful—went with me everywhere and paid for everything. But it wasn't what I wanted. On the other side, I have Bob. He wants a quiet wedding: just our families in the minister's living room. Between Bob and my mother, I'm about to go nuts."

She is in a hailstorm and it's all coming down on Becky's head.

Sometimes before the wedding is over some very rude things are said. Occasionally there are severe wounds among relatives.

If you have open-minded, cooperative parents, thank God for them twice.

The object of a wedding is to get married. Don't let it become an agony. Hang loose on the arrangements. They often are not worth the strain. If something about them really aggravates you, let it be known early. Tell yourselves repeatedly, "No set of candles, no corsage, and no wedding is worth hurting the two of us."

All hailstorms pass. Just don't let the pelting hurt anyone.

You can also expect a good rainstorm. Everything will become overcast, dull, and damp. Don't be surprised.

It is hard to keep a bubbling love during an engagement. Ron explained it to me this way. "Just let it happen. I'm tired of all the questions I ask myself. Is she the right one? Is this really love? Should we go through with this large wedding? Man, just let it happen. I'm numb."

He was suffering from engagement fatigue. Ron was tired, discouraged, gloomy. He was still in love but it was masked under all the prolonged pressure. As the saying goes—it was raining on his parade.

Don't interpret the doldrums as a lack of love. The barometric pressure is getting to you. You don't have as much zip on a cloudy day. Try to recall the evening before it became drawn out. Remember that evening alone in a restaurant? The glowing candles—the look on his face—the gentle touch of his hand? It will all be there again. The rain will pass. Everything will look brighter and greener. Don't let a few dips and doubts rattle you.

If all these other storms pass over, a thunderstorm will get you for sure—the kind that rumbles loudly and frightens everyone. It's just a passing noise, but it's still scary.

Are you really ready to live intimately with someone? This is a genuine fear. It disturbs a large number of engaged people. Maybe you have lived with brothers and sisters. Possibly you have had roommates. Marriage is a different dimension. Do you want someone to get to know you this closely?

Your partner is going to discover your personal habits. Do you snore? What about your hygiene? What if you aren't a good sexual partner? Can you compromise with your mate's life style? Does she go to bed early and you late? Can you stand each other's uncamouflaged temperament?

If you knew each other intimately and daily, would you continue to love each other? You can hear the fears rolling like thunder? Will this be something you can't handle?

These reservations are not abnormal. They will pass. In most cases, the better we know each other, the more we love each other.

"I know my wife's little habits now. I love them," one happy husband said.

Unless you have some bizarre or weird habit, the two of you will mesh beautifully. Do you eat raw onions in bed? Do you chew tobacco in church? If any of these are true of you, you have some adjustments to worry about.

Every year a million people become married and adjust well. Many of them stay married for fifteen, twenty-five, or forty years and have a great time. You will, too.

Don't let the rolling thunder scare you. When you get to know each other better you will love each other even more.

If you think you are the exception to this, you are not. We have amazing adaptability. Add love and it is marvelous what a couple can do. Despite whatever reservations you have, you are normal. Love really will win out.

Once when Jesus was out on the lake in a boat, a gigantic storm came up quickly. It threatened to destroy the vessel and everyone in it. He decided to speak to the storm.

"And he arose, and rebuked the wind, and said to the sea, Peace, be still. And the wind ceased, and there was a great calm" (Mark 4:39, KJV).

The storms of engagement can be just as threatening. Tell them to calm down. They can be destructive. The smart couples keep them to a minimum. They remind themselves that all storms pass. When they are over, life goes on with tremendous happiness.

Not every engagement is worth redeeming. Some couples have constant and irreversible storms. They really should bail out—immediately. It is too bad to have to say that, but it is true.

However, most engagements are worth the effort. I see too many couples at the breaking point for no good reason. They heard a rumor. They have picked up some lousy advice. It isn't the magic cloud they thought it was. They are tired. Eventually they go their separate ways thinking the marriage was never for them. Maybe it wasn't. But maybe they lost something just because they became confused.

One of my favorite couples, two college students, were so enjoyable and interesting I think of them often. We got together several times because their engagement was on the rocks. They loved each other—neither denied it. They had fun together. It was obvious.

What was their problem? She had heard a sermon someplace and he didn't live up to it. The minister had said if a young man is this or that, don't marry him. She took the minister's opinion as gospel.

Then her sister said you should never marry a man if he won't do this or that. She loved her sister and that advice really bothered her.

Here were two excellent Christian young people being torn apart for no good reason. It was a thrill to see them finally get married.

Engagement can be a dizzy elevator. It's a passing part of life. It will usher you into a beautiful marriage.

3

GOOD PEOPLE MAKE
GOOD MARRIAGES

Marriage solves almost no problems. This sentence should be printed at the top of every marriage certificate. Too many look at marriage like baking soda: it can do practically anything. It is important to know what it can and can't accomplish before the organ starts playing. Marriage offers some basic joys. You will have someone who cares. Loneliness will be diminished. Sexual pleasure will be available but with several frustrations. These and other benefits should not be minimized.

However, most personal and personality problems will be intensified and not eliminated in marriage. If you expect wedding bells to cure your hangups, back up and look again.

Good people make good marriages. The more you can smooth off your rough edges now, the greater chance the two of you have for tremendous happiness.

Someone has a terrible temper, but his love-struck partner rationalizes. After they get married she will be able to calm him down. Don't bet your marriage on it. In most cases the temper will stay. Many times it will become worse in a close situation.

This isn't being said to frighten couples. It has to be said to help us face reality. The first few months after marriage will probably be bubbling joy. Then your personalities will settle into their normal tempo. Both of you will begin to revert to your real behavior. If you married a good person he will be exactly that. If you unite with an unsteady personality, he will revert almost immediately.

Don't fool yourself into believing your partner will become Mr. Nice-Guy. He will be basically what he is now.

Ask yourself once more. If your partner never changes at all, can you be happy with him? Don't get married until you answer that question.

There was a young man whom everyone liked. He was intelligent, had a great sense of humor. People were drawn to him. Greg became engaged to a most unpleasant character. He loved her and rationalized Ellen's behavior. After all, she was under a great deal of pressure. Between going to school and planning a wedding, she was bound to become irritable.

Greg's friends never mentioned it, but they stayed away more and more. Ellen was genuinely unbearable.

One year after their marriage they filed for divorce. Greg's hopes were not based in fact. Marriage could not change Ellen. It only intensified her characteristics.

The formula has almost mathematical precision. Selfish fiancés make selfish husbands. Insecure fiancées make insecure wives. Don't fantasize that you are marrying someone you are not.

All of us know someone who has been tremendously changed by marriage. I think of a man who married an outstanding woman. She changed him all for the better. His clothes changed, he joined a bowling league, became a leader in several organizations, and enjoyed life far more.

These were things he always wanted to do, but he couldn't get off the ground. His personality is still the same. He was a good person and still is.

Marriage is a normal part of life. Sometimes we talk as if it were different. If you are a kind person, considerate, sharing, a good listener, and feel good about yourself, your chances for a sound marriage are excellent. But these are the same qualities which make solid people. Marriage is not a separate world.

Divorce courts are filled with couples who married to solve problems: She wanted to get away from her parents. He was dependent on a bottle. She was a manic depressive. He couldn't control his passions. They thought marriage was the cure.

One of the saddest women I ever met was one who had married for money. Not big money as most of us might imagine. She was just looking for simple support. Her health wasn't good and she felt she couldn't work. She met a lonely man, and a marriage of "convenience" seemed like a great solution. Before long she wished she was in the bread line at a street mission.

This isn't being written to frighten you (well, maybe some of you). Rather it is a call for us to take a close look at ourselves as well as our partners.

We can be changed. We can change ourselves and God can change us. The more good alterations we make before we are married the better are the chances for a healthy union. Read that again.

A young lady said to me in defiance, "I can't help it. I am what I am." Thank God that isn't true.

Read this verse slowly to yourself: "When someone becomes a Christian he becomes a brand new person inside. He is not the same any more. A new life has begun!" (2 Cor. 5:17).

The potential for change is there. Some of those adjustments can be made by our own determination. A couple may need professional attention. You may have to ask God to ship in a few miracles directly.

A solid marriage is not dependent on your ability to be perfect. However, the smoother your machine is running, the better the factory will go.

Here are some starter questions. Add your own to this short sample.

How do you handle anger? Do you brood until everyone around you is uncomfortable and depressed? Are you the other extreme? Do you have to break things, hit people, or put on a physical performance? Do you have to hold on to it for days or even weeks? Either extreme will take its toll on a relationship. Practice talking about your anger and keep short accounts of it. Never let it carry over into the next day (Eph. 4:26).

For years we have practiced harmful behavior. Today let us start practicing constructive behavior.

Do you get more fun out of giving or getting? A healthy person likes to receive. To have one partner completely deny himself makes a one-sided marriage. However, if we see our major goal as getting, we establish a self-centered relationship. This will become painful later.

Practice giving more than you get. What is your main concern at Christmas; what you will give or what you will receive? After you have been married a year, this attitude will make an enormous difference (Acts 20:35).

Do you have to win? Does it tear you up when things don't go your way? Look at the little things in your life. How do you feel if you lose a game of "Password" or "Scrabble"?

A young wife said, "We have learned not to play games together. My husband can't stand to lose. If I beat him he's impossible to live with."

Maybe you take yourself too seriously. It is no fun to share with someone who must always be right. This is a good definition of spoiled. You can change that by relaxing and learning to appreciate sharing. Love does not demand its own way (1 Cor. 13:5).

How do you get along with jealousy? When your partner gets compliments, does it tear you up or make you happy? What will happen if your wife has a job making more money than you? Do you become upset when your partner does things with his friends?

Suppose your wife wanted to join a women's bowling league? What if your husband wanted to play on a local basketball team? Since you can't participate, will you insist your partner not go either? Will you let him go but pout about it for a week?

Your reactions now will give you a good clue. Are you jealous and overly possessive today? Unless you practice letting go, your smothering will continue into marriage (Jas. 3:15, 16). Don't confuse jealousy with love.

Are you a trusting person? This can be hard, especially if your parents have had trouble. Do you want to carry this feeling into your outstanding relationship?

Possibly you feel insecure. You are constantly afraid you will lose everything. Some have made this part of their personality. They don't trust anything which is going well. If life is running smoothly, they are certain tragedy is about to hit. They expect trouble. By expecting it they frequently cause it.

If your partner calls to cancel a date, do you distrust her reasons? When she says she loves you, are you suspicious that she is pretending?

Feelings of distrust are understandable, especially if you have been hurt often. However, you must begin to improve your trust. Love calls for us to completely accept our partner. The degree to which we refuse to trust is the exact degree to which we will fracture our relationship.

Talk to your partner about your feelings of distrust. Your partner may be able to put it to rest bit by bit (Prov. 31:10, 11).

Check out your sense of humor. This sounds easy because everyone believes he has one. Can you laugh at yourself? If not, you just flunked. Do other people do funny and strange things, but not you? If not, perhaps you take yourself too seriously.

When your partner messes up, that humor will become even more important. What will happen when she burns dinner? Will you throw a fit? Make a speech? Or comfort her?

Some of the best marriages have partners who can laugh at themselves. It will really come in handy one day when you are broke, the car radiator leaks, and your favorite chair breaks.

Practice laughing; it is good medicine. Flatly refuse to marry anyone who cannot be cheerful and laugh at himself (Prov. 17:22). Flatly.

Make your own list of rough edges. What would you like to smooth out? What changes or improvements would you most like to see in your partner? Now is the time to start working.

In premarital counseling I always try to ask, "If you could change one thing in your partner, what would it be?" Almost every time this question brings good response. "He always wants me to make the decisions." "She puts me down a lot." "He always talks about old girl friends." "She asks questions and won't let me answer."

Try it with your partner. Each of you agree to share one or two things you would like to change in each other or yourself. Then make suggestions on how you can help.

It sounds great to say, "I wouldn't change one hair on your head." All right, leave her hairdo alone, but a couple of trait changes might be good insurance on your marriage success. You are doing both a fantastic favor.

What kind of person would you like to be? If you could map out the type of personality you want most, where would you start? Why not start there? Tell yourself three things you are not doing as well as you would like. Now aim for those goals. As you move toward them you will become happier with yourself. In the end both of you will be happier with your marriage.

Knowledge alone cannot make a compatible marriage. Learning about married life in itself is not enough. After you read the books and take the counseling one question remains all important. What kind of person are you? No amount of information will overcome a failure here.

Experts in social behavior are deep into theories of what ruins marriages. Is it a mobile society? Working women? Urbanization? Confused roles? Financial pressure? Unrealistic sex expectations? Close living quarters?

One authority would have none of this. Cutting through all the dialogue, he said simply, "Basically people are getting divorced because of selfishness."

Could it be that simple? A common human weakness as basic as this? Marriage is made up of people. People with good qualities make good marriages.

In the past we have been guilty of sex prejudice. The job of changing has always been relegated to women. The male supposedly had an inalienable right to be whatever he was. A husband's personality was considered fixed. If the wife did not fit into his puzzle, it was her place to change until she matched.

Thank God, that day is ending. No longer does he make the sole decision on where to live. No longer does he alone set the pace of their social life. No longer does he invest the family money without even consulting his spouse.

To consider your wife's feelings in making decisions was once considered a sign of weakness. If he was a man, he would tell her what to do. If she was a good woman, she would obey.

Do you want to marry a man who must prove his manhood by bossing his wife around? If he needs this, how fragile is his manhood?

The biblical concept is not this rigid. It offers choices to the female which we are only now starting to admit. Read about the virtuous woman in Proverbs 31. She is a woman who has more liberty than most husbands today are willing to allow. The virtuous wife runs a business. "She goes out to inspect a field, and buys it" (v. 16). Don't marry until your partner has read this chapter slowly.

A good partner is not afraid to give his wife freedom. Let her express herself. What interests will mean the most to her life? Would working outside the home be healthy for her and your family? A sensitive partner does not try to map out his spouse's life and nail it down.

I can remember a first-class couple who were shooting sparks over the issue of freedom. First, he told his story.

At the end of a day he was tired, ready for a hot meal. If he wanted to go out, watch television, or work a puzzle he expected his wife to be available. After all, this is why he got married.

33

That sounded simple enough. It's the same principle we have been working on for hundreds of years.

Marie also had a point and her husband wasn't really considering it. She wanted more than to be lost in her husband's personality. Her part-time job gave her a sense of added worth. The two organizations she belonged to gave her the chance to contribute.

How much freedom can you allow your partner? How much freedom do you want? Do your marriage a favor and discuss this soon.

It isn't just a question of the wife accommodating her husband. Can the husband also accommodate his wife? The first rule of submission is submitting to each other (Eph. 5:21). The second rule is for wives to submit to their husbands (v. 22).

If there is a split decision, a husband must make the final call. However, before the last word is in, a wife has every right to include her feelings and opinions. A smart, sensitive husband will not ignore them.

A marriage relationship has to be based on affection and consideration. It isn't like running a factory or a schoolyard.

This is why a fifty-fifty marriage is a poor concept. It says, "I'll do my half if you do your half." All this does is draw the line at which you will fight. It defines limits but is without compassion.

Far better is a 100 percent-100 percent marriage in which each partner says, "I'm going to give this my all." Mature partners aren't afraid of this type of commitment because they both love and trust each other.

You are not afraid to give your all to your mate. You are confident your partner will do the same.

It helps a great deal to marry someone who is not only the throb of your heart but also your friend. Naturally you need other friends, also. If your spouse is not also your friend she will soon become a mere domestic companion. A domestic companion shares your interest in a house, children, and payments. A friend is interested in the other aspects of your life which circle outside your house.

I was fortunate to marry my best friend. (But not my only one.) It is easy to confirm this. If I could spend an evening talking to anyone, I know who my first choice would be: my wife.

There is an old French proverb which tells us: Select a partner you can talk to intelligently for the next fifty years.

Sometime when you are asking yourself what kind of a partner you will make, read 1 Corinthians 13:4-7. It is the world's greatest description of love. Take a brief survey of what love does and apply it to your coming marriage.

Love is patient. It doesn't push a partner where he doesn't want to go. Love waits while his spouse thinks things over. It knows when it shouldn't bring up a problem.

Love is kind. Its behavior is gentle. Love doesn't believe being coarse or crude is cute. It not only hears what is said, it also hears what is meant.

Love is not jealous. When your spouse beats you in bowling, you are glad for her. When someone shakes her hand, you are as happy as if the person were shaking yours. (Besides, you will beat her next time.)

Love is not proud. It doesn't have to puff up like a frog. If she disagrees and selects the wrong road, he doesn't rub it in. Love doesn't crow when it's right.

Love is not selfish. He calls home when he knows he will be late. Love withholds its sex drive when the time isn't right. Love lets her pick out the wallpaper—then he praises it.

Love is not rude. It remembers how to say thank you. Love helps pick up the paper clips your partner dropped. Love never talks over your spouse's conversations. It never answers for your mate. It never jokes in a way aimed to hurt your partner.

Love doesn't demand its own way. Love is mature enough to give in. It goes to eat at the restaurant she likes best. Then he eats like he loves it. He waits quietly while his partner shops. (At least for the first hour.)

Love is not irritated and touchy. It doesn't have a trigger temper. He listens to criticism. She can take some friendly kidding. Love doesn't boil at every mother-in-law joke.

Love doesn't hold grudges. It has no notebook to write down accounts. After the problem has been discussed, love never brings it up again. After an argument, love always rubs feet in bed at night.

Love isn't happy when its partner is hurt. It isn't glad when its partner gets chewed out. Love isn't happy when a friend criticizes its partner. Love wants to see her win.

Love is loyal. Love doesn't tear down, it builds. It knows she was wrong and hugs her anyway. When love has nothing good to say, it stays quiet.

Love always believes. In a difference it always believes its partner first. Love is blind and is glad it is. If your mate says she was kidnapped by a flying saucer, love asks how high she was taken.

Love expects the best. When dinner isn't ready, love assumes its partner couldn't help it. When he comes home late, love knows he was up to good. Love wants to believe you threw out his old shirt by mistake.

Love never fails. Money, youth, and motorboats all fail. Waistlines stretch, teeth vanish, eyes weaken. Skin wrinkles, heads bald, arches drop. Love and love alone never gives up.

Love is profound and simple at the same time. Marriage isn't so complicated if we apply basic human love. The same qualities which make a good person make a good marriage.

4
CHANGING RELATIONSHIPS

Marriage is change. Most of the changes will be for the better and you will enjoy them. A few will hurt, but they have to be made. To expect and accept these changes in relationship is a good indication you are mature enough to marry. If you try to keep every relationship with friends and parents the same as before, you are in for an explosion.

You are going to get to know your partner more intimately than anyone you have known before. You haven't known a brother, sister, friend, or parent this closely. Not only are you going to be united physically, but also mentally and emotionally. In a few years you will find yourselves thinking alike. Often you will know what your mate is going to say before he says it. When she hurts, your heart will break. When she succeeds, your heart will leap with joy. That's fantastic. If you think you are melting into one now, just check a few years away. Many couples even start to look alike.

This is part of the greatness of marriage. When you are around a beautiful person, some of that beauty rubs off. It has to, just from the fallout. If you married an ugly personality, after a while you start to pick up the uglies.

Personality changes personality. Thank God. That is why he injected so many good people into our lives.

This is why you are marrying someone with humility. If you marry a person who is stuck on himself, he doesn't appreciate change. Since he is already perfect, he sees no need for alterations.

Only fools marry brick walls. They are immovable and cannot be improved. Brick walls expect you to change to match their personality.

The smart partner knows his mate is good for him. He goes into marriage saying, "Marriage will change me. I am ready to make changes and improve." If he says this, throw an arm lock on him and take him directly to the altar.

Because marriage is change there is one scene you can almost bet on. Somewhere down the line (and maybe not far) you will be sitting in a corner sucking your thumb. You will be saying to yourself, "I always have to give in. I change 90 percent of the time and she only changes 10 percent."

This type of thumb pacification is also known as self-pity. Expect it. It comes and goes. Normally it is a tremendous exaggeration, but don't be surprised.

If you move a train east from Des Moines toward Chicago two changes have to happen. You become closer to Chicago but farther from Des Moines. You cannot become closer to Chicago and remain close to Des Moines at the same time. The same fact exists in marriage. An intimate relationship with my new partner will change the close relationships with my old friends.

For a year I had a close relationship with an excellent friend. We were both single, had a great deal of open time, and floated around together. Don and I would go to the beach, eat out, or just bum around. The minute he was married, that relationship had to change He no longer had the open time. There was now a new and outstand ing personality in his life. If we had kept that close a relationship it would have been at the expense of his new marriage. To get closer to Chicago he had to move away from Des Moines.

This was a healthy, normal change.

Paul was the opposite. He had two close friends and the trio owned a racing car. It was a demanding hobby. They raced twice a week and worked on the blue bomb three other nights.

When Paul married he stayed in Des Moines. He visited Chicago. He even kept his luggage there and dropped in for meals. But there was no doubt where his real home was. Paul wanted his marriage partner to be a satellite—to orbit around his world. There would be no melting of personalities.

This is not the type of change most of us want. It is terribly unhealthy

As always, the Bible holds this change in excellent balance. In marriage she becomes more like him and he becomes more like her. The two change to become one.

"That the husband and wife are one body is proved by the Scripture which says, 'A man must leave his father and mother when he marries, so that he can be perfectly joined to his wife, and the two shall be one'" (Eph. 5:31).

If you marry someone who is not mature enough to expect change, you are buying into an Excedrin headache. Read that again.

This doesn't mean you have to throw all of your old friends off the back of a train. Frequently, you keep some old friends and add new ones. It merely means adjustments have to be made.

Two types of friends are couple-crushers. The first is the close friend who demands all of your time and energy. Your new partner takes absolute priority. Old friends must be pared down to size

Your new mate must feel free from competition. If you consistently would rather be with old friends more than her, she will become puzzled.

The second couple-crusher is the personality conflict. Once in a while an old friend will drive a new mate into spasms. The offense could be his conversation, clothes, body odor, feet on the coffee table, or any other of thousands. If your mate cannot cope, then your course is clear. Your old friend has to be controlled or eventually eliminated. Often it will happen naturally. Sometimes it has to be encouraged.

Maybe you can keep all your old friends. Terrific. A few can. The important thing is to tell yourself up front: My new relationship is more important to me than any other in life. I will let no other relationship hurt this one. If I do I am a fool.

This leads us to former girl friends and boyfriends. Where do they fit in this new picture?

In almost all cases they don't fit.

There are exceptions. I hear of an old girl friend who becomes the new wife's best friend. I also hear of someone's finding a paper bag filled with one hundred dollar bills. It seems that I hear of both equally often.

One rule of thumb can be used concerning keeping old flames around: Don't. It is too difficult for both new partners to handle the situation well. Most often your mate will feel threatened by your old flame. Not always—only 999 times out of 1,000. When this doesn't happen the reverse often does. You start leaning too much on your former heartthrob.

I know one man who keeps an old girl friend close. She has never gotten over him, so it is no simple friendship. He loves the attention and uses his girl friend or his wife to get whatever he wants. There is probably no sexual activity between the husband and his old flame—just excessive attention. All three of them need their clocks checked.

It not only is unwise to have old flames *around*. Most mates aren't thrilled at *hearing* about them either. Some husbands enjoy describing old girl friends. This can be cruel sport. The smart partner doesn't bring them up. Your mate probably wants to know who they were. Maybe he wants details. However, it is certain he doesn't want too much information and absolutely not too often.

Live in the present. The past probably wasn't as interesting as you imagine it anyway.

Chuck was one young man who had to make a tough decision. He had an old friend who happened to be female. There was never anything serious between the two except that they were real pals. Several girl friends came and went but Michelle was always there.

After Chuck was married, Michelle continued to write and the contact seemed harmless to both of them. It wasn't harmless to Chuck's bride. When Michelle offered to come and visit, it was more than the bride could handle. Chuck loved his wife too much to hurt her. He knew he had to back off from the relationship with Michelle.

Relationships change in marriage. They must always change in one direction—to reassure love and unity.

What is the most difficult of the changing relationships? The hardest change—bar none—concerns our parents and in-laws. Consistently this is a major problem among married couples. It is hard to switch from being a dependent into an independent.

First, stop and give a silent salute to the thousands who have no trouble here. There are some terrific parent-couple compliments. Don't believe all the jokes you hear. Some couples would not trade their parents for anything.

If we start to accept all the stereotypes, they have a way of coming true. By expecting trouble we often cause it.

The parents who seem to get along the best are the ones who have this basic principle in line: they raised their child to get rid of him. This is the purpose of having children. Those who raised children to keep them have created puppets with tight strings.

The smart parents have moved the young person along steadily. They have given the youth increased freedom as he has grown. Their hold has become less and less choking. They have been aiming for the day when he will be free and flying on his own.

They have understood the Scriptures well. "A man must leave his father and mother when he marries" (Eph. 5:31a). When the time came, everyone was prepared for him to leave.

Jim and Nancy had just this type of marriage. They felt fortunate to not live too close to either parent. They could visit but were not continuously camped on each other's doorstep. If they asked their parents for advice, they could usually get it. Sometimes the parents politely refused even then. They merely assured Jim and Nancy that either way they did it would be perfectly fine with them.

The parents were helpful and friendly. They had no desire to butt in even once. If they were going to make a mistake, it would be from holding back.

Jim and Nancy have only appreciation for parents. They don't quite understand what other couples are complaining about.

A healthy parental relationship is possible. It just isn't done often enough.

One of the saddest young women I know has never been set free. Today she is married and has three children. After years of training she also has an excellent career. Yet, if you know her, one thing becomes obvious. Everything she does is aimed at pleasing her mother. She keeps a spotless house, dresses impeccably, keeps the children completely under tow. There is nothing wrong with any of these things except that she lives in constant fear of her mother. Any derogatory remark from Mom and she crumbles. Mother has never set her free and never intends to. Cindy's husband also lives daily with the ghost of a living mother.

Resolve to avoid the same mistake. Raise your children to get rid of them.

We are discussing a parent problem and not just an in-law problem. Often we imagine it is an in-law problem because we do not see our own parents as clearly. If our parents do something wrong we are likely to be more understanding. We have seen them this way before and have learned to accept it. When our mate's parents do the same thing, we object.

Keep the perspective sharp. It is a parent problem.

Since it is a parent problem, the solution needs to be between parent and child. If your parents are making life miserable for your mate, it is better if you talk to your parents. Don't expect your partner to correct his in-laws. Crossing those lines usually only adds to the hostilities.

The hottest spot in the parent problem is between a mother and her son's mate. The hot wires which hit the most are female. I am not bigoted; that is just a fact.

Even this is not an in-law problem. The son should resolve this either by talking to his mother or his partner. It isn't reasonable to expect the wife to correct her mother-in-law. The mother has no business correcting her daughter-in-law.

Expect to have a great relationship with each other's parents. If you look for a fantastic experience, you are far more likely to get one.

The smart couple will pledge to keep a few simple guidelines.

Never live with parents unless one or both of you are in a wheelchair. Even then, try not to do it.

Margaret agrees now. When she first got married they were both broke, but in love. They got married and moved in with her parents. She told me, "Tell couples not to do it. It just doesn't work."

If you can't afford to set up housekeeping, you can't afford to get married. It doesn't take much money to become one. Live modestly, but live alone.

Don't accept gifts with strings. Parents like to be kind. We have two beautiful chairs in our living room which were a gift from Pat's mother. We have great parents. But *never* have they tried to tell us how to raise our children. They don't even suggest what we do with our lives.

Wayne had the opposite experience.

"Sure, I don't like what her parents say. They are always screaming about how we treat the kids. They don't like what I do for a living. But what can I say? They have given us every appliance in the house."

What could he say? Don't get yourself into that wedge. Some kindnesses are terribly cruel.

Don't dump on parents. Many parents never asked for this. We borrow money from them. We park our kids at their house. We carry off half their furniture and their popcorn popper. Then we throw up our hands and scream, "Why don't they stay out of our lives?"

I have talked to good parents who didn't ask for this. Their children follow them around like a cloud and then complain about being smothered.

You're too smart to do that.

Change is almost always difficult. The change in our relationship to our parents is no exception. One day you belonged to your parents. Today you don't. The transition isn't easy.

In most marriages there are six personalities directly affected: a couple and four parents. In order for the crossover to be smooth, all half-dozen must accept it equally. That's asking a lot.

This is the reason why the Bible said it four times. When a person gets married, he leaves his parents.

The majority of us grew up learning to obey our parents. Some were more successful than others. Still, this was the theme. It was correct and helpful. How does this relationship change when we become married? Obey drops out, but honor remains.

"Children, obey your parents; this is the right thing to do because God has placed them in authority over you. Honor your father and mother. This is the first of God's Ten Commandments that ends with a promise" (Eph. 6:1, 2).

Honor is respect. If our parents have advice or counsel to give, we appreciate it. Their experience is valuable and we are foolish not to listen. Wisdom is a gift usually reserved for those with years behind them. There are times when we will seek out their advice. This could save us a carload of agony.

The line is drawn when it comes to the question of obedience. A partner who doesn't understand this is not completely ready to marry.

When you marry, you do not marry an entire family. You marry each other. Other relatives become satellites, but they are not part of the marriage. Only two people become one, not six or a dozen.

Ann was a typical victim of "marrying" a family. When she stopped by to see me she was on her way to pack. Her husband, Dale, was completely tied to his parents. He still believed he had to obey them.

Both of Dale's parents were healthy. They worked every day and attended social functions. Mother wanted the family at their home on Sundays. Dad wanted Dale to help him work on Saturdays and a couple of evenings a week. Whenever Ann tried to change this routine Dale became hot There was no way he could go against his parents' wishes.

Dale wasn't really ready to get married. He expected Ann to marry an entire family and melt her identity into them. Now she was looking for luggage.

If you marry someone who has not cut the cord, you will spend many days mumbling to yourself. To become separated from your parents is neither unloving nor inconsiderate. It's natural. It is maturing. It is beautiful.

Smart parents store up for themselves. Not just financially, but in every area. They develop their own interests, hobbies, friends, and emotional support. When their children leave, these parents are not gutted. Their lives and happiness were not entirely dependent on their children. The families which are built mainly on child-satisfaction are heading for a letdown.

Whatever the level of changing relationships, they can be exciting. Above all else, they are normal and healthy. Each one is a stepping stone in the rich maturing of your life.

5

THE FUN OF MARRYING A STRANGER

How do you like adventure? Do you find it stimulating, even exciting? Do you see something new as interesting or as a threat?

Marriage may be life's greatest safari. An amazing trip into a new territory filled with beauty, wonder, and change. The attitude you take into this trip will make a fantastic difference.

The two of you have taken time to get to know each other. By now you have a fair idea of what makes your partner tick. Immediately after you are married you will begin to unfold the rest of the map. You won't like every side road and gully you see, but most of it will be everything you hoped for. This rule far outweighs the exceptions.

Why do you want to marry this character, anyway? Have you ever thought of why you two strangers decided to get together?

One group of surveys says you picked each other because opposites attract. You are going to get married because you are different. Another battery of surveys says you gravitated toward each other because you are similar. This is handy. You can select either group you want and agree with it.

The fact is, marriage makes a lousy science. If nine people out of ten marry because of loneliness, you could be one of the nine, or you could be the one. Don't try to study marriage to death.

Why did you select the mate you plan to marry? What is attractive about him physically? Which part of his personality do you find most appealing? There is no special key which applies to everyone. Your key is like no one else's.

Sometimes two extroverts make the worst possible partners. They may be always screaming and stomping out on each other. The next two extroverts may be as happy as two penguins on a one-foot ice drift.

We do not have to pair off into extroverts and introverts. Don't fall for the old "Type A cannot be happy with Type B" formula. Too many young people have missed magnificent partners because they believed these "magic" guidelines.

Our basic premise remains unchanged. The same qualities which make good people make good marriages.

Some marriages are terrible from day one. Every young couple needs to admit this. A couple came to talk about getting married. It was obvious that they were a mismatch. It wasn't because of introvert-extrovert conflicts—the male lacked the qualities essential to a good person. He was inconsiderate, demanding, paranoid, gruff, and self-centered. He was not just flunking marriage—he was flunking humanity.

Later he had marital problems. Baloney. He had humanity problems and it was affecting his marriage.

Is this stranger you are about to marry a good person? Pack your fears away. Good people make good marriages.

There used to be an old adage floating around which insisted: Don't marry people from broken homes. The theory was that it was a chain reaction of broken homes breaking homes. This is true only if people are statistics and categories. Fortunately, we are flesh, blood, brains, and nerve endings.

I know tons of good people who come from broken homes. Don't fall for prejudices and stereotypes. Christians should be the first people to see past these blinders.

Some young people have lost beautiful potential partners because they listened to nonsense. Their Aunt Agnes always said you should never marry a man whose parents are divorced. Mom says I should look for a quiet man because I talk all the time. Anyone who marries a foreigner will regret it.

Mark them all false. You are people, not statistics.

The doors of marriage will swing open and the two of you will go waltzing in wide-eyed, eager, and flexible. You'll find you can hardly wait to discover new things about the person you love. With this attitude you can't go wrong.

Begin on day one to make a depth chart on your mate. Recently

I saw a depth chart on the Chesapeake Bay. It is easy to see the shallow spots to avoid when sailing. You can just as readily note the deep places where you can sail ahead.

Over a time these depths will change. Sand will shift and new paths be worn away. Mark these down in your mind also.

Making a depth chart is not the same as conniving. There is nothing deceptive about it. Anyone who has worked for a boss has done the same thing. When the boss is in a foul mood, everyone stays clear. If he is telling jokes, they crowd in with requests.

There will be certain high or low points in your mate's day. A smart partner mentally charts them. There are some situations which he dreads. A good navigator backs off when she sees her partner getting near those. Good mates read the charts well. They sail more smoothly and go aground less often.

One partner was always frustrated. She got home an hour before her new husband. During that time she drank a cup of coffee, started supper, and often arranged her evening.

At six o'clock the light of her life came dragging in the door, looking like a wet raincoat. Glad to see him, she came on like a game show host. How was his day? Did he want to see her new shoes? Could he go with her later to the shopping center?

Her bowed-back beau always seemed so negative. He didn't want to see anything and he didn't want to go anywhere. Sometimes she felt sorry for herself for marrying such a deadpan grouch.

One day the facts hit her like a mosquito in a motorcycle race. After dinner he was pleasant, conversant, and practically creative.

She realized she had one hour ahead of him to gather her wits and energize. She marked it on her depth chart. Six o'clock is a sandy reef. Wait until the craft is further from shore.

Some partners will find evening breezes the best. The two of you are sitting in the living room and all the necessary things are done. It is easy to talk without tension. Calmer decisions can be made.

The next couple will find those evening chats the pits. It's late. Your mate doesn't think straight. Don't try to solve inflation, the oil crisis, or the bank overdraft now.

Most partners can mark this on their chart immediately. Don't give bad news late at night. Sometimes it can't be helped; but when you can, hold it.

If the transmission falls out of the car, midnight is probably not a great hour to shock him. If there is a gas leak in the basement, any hour is a good one to tell. When there is a choice for bad news, don't pick late.

Timing is only the beginning of this chart. My wife and I play a game over baked potatoes. She likes them, I don't. They are so easy to fix, Pat manages to slip them in once in a while.

By now she has learned the ground rules. If she has done me a special favor during the day, I can count on a baked potato. (This is the severest form of cruelty.) What else can I do but smile and try to push the spud down?

This is clearly unfair. But she has learned she can sail here when the wind is right.

Charting your partner is not the old female slave concept. This approach said the wife had to knuckle under and do whatever the husband wanted.

This outlook on marriage is dying and never should have been alive. The wife-as-slave idea was never biblical. The husband was to make decisions only when the two partners could not agree. The wife was never intended to be wallpaper (Eph. 5:21, 22; Prov. 31).

Charting is absolutely a two-way street. She takes soundings on him and he takes soundings on her.

For instance, husbands can mark down a day or two of low tide each month. Most wives sag during their menstrual period. Learn to chart this by experience. Women are extremely different. One wife will barely flinch during it. Other women can be bedridden.

The biggest help is to communicate. All a wife has to say is, "This is a bad time of the month for me." It can prevent many problems. Husband then knows to back off for a couple of days. Without this information some strong arguments often erupt.

At the bottom of your imaginary chart, wives should write this note: "Most male illnesses are terminal." There are exceptions to this rule, but they are too rare to consider.

Many men can't stand being sick. When the flu knocks them out for a couple of days they become impossible. He is convinced he is going to die. He tells his wife where the insurance policies are hidden. He calls for the chroniclers to record his last words.

For many young wives this is a startling experience. Husbands will expect to be babied, fed, and flooded with attention. They frequently fall into lapses of self-pity. Somehow men can't imagine Roger Staubach with diarrhea.

Ride this storm out patiently. Your neighbor goes through the same thing.

In most cases we marry people who operate on different levels. Our mate will probably talk at a rate different from us. Don't try to remake the person. Learn to appreciate him. Silence has its healthy qualities and we can see its value by watching our partner. Great conversation can be rich medicine. Listen to your mate and appreciate its strength.

As time does its work, many couples become more like each other. The one will probably become more talkative and the other slightly more pensive. But don't force it. Learn to love the difference rather than demand imitation. A mature partner doesn't need to insist on compliance. She understands the need for personal freedom and variety.

John told me about his timing problem and how he matured. He was the type who loved to stay up late. Too much sleep drove him goofy. A good book or a late show were his idea of a relaxing evening.

His wife Lori acted as if electricity was evil. Why would anyone want to stay up late? If the sun went to bed, people were supposed to soon follow.

Their experience is common. During the first month both partners break down the stairs trying to get to bed early. It isn't that they are sleepy. As time passes, their normal patterns start to level off. Often the partners do not have the same sleep pattern. Trying to change frequently leads to frustration or haggling.

John and Lori decided it was smarter to chart each other than to fight. Lori now goes to bed at 10. They kiss good night and part happily. At midnight John climbs the stairs at his own pace.

They now mix respect and compliance. On some nights John goes to bed early. The next night Lori might stay up a little longer. Frequently John will go to bed and make love and then get up for an hour.

Each married a stranger, but they are getting along fantastically. Instead of saying, "Happiness is to be like me," they have charted each other. Now they do it their own way and each other's way.

This is called marriage.

Men have traditionally found this harder to accept than women. Many of us thought women were to make depth charts on us, but men never made charts on women. After all, the purpose of marriage was to make the husband deliriously happy.

The entire society is maturing. Now we know the purpose in marriage is to please each other. Men will be charting women and not the other way only.

This isn't a new concept. The Bible taught it thousands of years ago.

"And you husbands, show the same kind of love to your wives as Christ showed to the church when he died for her" (Eph. 5:25).

Old King Nebuchadnezzar understood the principle. He greatly loved the woman who owned his heart. After they got married he noticed she was becoming melancholy. Her vim and vigor were gone. After he patiently inquired, she finally told him the facts. The new queen missed the beautiful mountains of her home country. She didn't know if she could ever get used to the dry plains of Babylon.

The great romantic went right to work. He ordered mountains built. They were to be near the palace and have gigantic trees and lush gardens. The king would set his lover's heart singing or break the national budget trying.

Nebuchadnezzar's little valentine became one of the wonders of the world—the Hanging Gardens of Babylon. All because he gave his heart to a little girl from the hills.

Make yourself a promise before you begin to chart your partner. Promise you will never brood over the changes you make. Some foolish partners make sacrifices for their mate and then spend years pouting about it. Love which is grudging is not love at all.

If a man agrees to buy a house in the suburbs because it's his wife's dream, he cannot then turn it into a weapon. For years he brings it up whenever there is a disagreement. After a couple of seasons of being beaten over the head by a house, the old domicile loses some of its luster.

Sometimes generosity is more painful than denial. The person inflicting the misery usually can't see it. He says, "Well, I gave her what she wanted, didn't I?" No! No! Not if it was given like a vice, to be slowly tightened around her heart until it aches continuously.

Giving in is an act of love, but if done incorrectly, it is cruel.

The Bible lays out a beautiful pattern for giving in. It says God loves a cheerful giver. It can also be translated "a giggling giver" (2 Cor. 9:7). Be a *hilarious* giver. Would this make you happy? Baby, this is just what I want you to have.

When you give gifts, there are several guidelines to keep. We want to give in love and not just in awkward patches. Give each gift this quick test.

1. Give what your mate wants, not what you want. Giving can be terribly selfish.

One year I gave my wife a baseball glove for Mother's Day. It was a charming act on my part, but I could be accused of selfishness. Fortunately, she understood how badly I needed someone to hit fly balls to.

Selfish giving takes some of the shine off the gift.

2. Gifts are not trades. There is a place to barter in marriage, but gift-giving is not it. You may strike a deal on vacations. You will spend one week in Florida and one week in Cleveland. That is a fair deal.

Don't make every gift a deal—it then ceases to be a gift. You give to your partner whether you will receive in return or not. (Strangely, this type of giving always receives.)

3. Give a nice gift. Your partner has been asking for a camera and you are tired of hearing about it. Don't buy a cheap one to get her off your back. Make her even happier than she had hoped.

Never give a gift with a twist of defiance.

4. Be that happy giver. Nothing increases the value of a gift as much as a warm, genuine smile.

Too many of us grew up with brothers and sisters. We learned how to give and in-fight at the same time. Marrying a magnificent stranger may call for a realignment of our emotions.

Promise your new partner you will give him plenty of room for creative breathing. Not only is this person a stranger to you, but he is in many ways a stranger to himself. There are many areas in which your mate has never ventured. He would like to. Whenever possible, encourage him to branch out.

Some partners are extremely proud that their mate never differs from them. There is no creative breathing. She thinks like him, acts like him, even enjoys the same shows. This can be good as long as one of them has not erased his personality.

A few years ago there was an important issue on the ballot in our town. A handsome new museum was built by private contributions, but there was no one to support it. We were asked to vote on whether or not the county should assume the cost.

The day of reckoning came. I voted to support it. My wife voted against. The measure failed.

What was the sense of voting? All we did was cancel each other out. But it was terribly important. She felt free to breathe her way and I breathed mine.

She chooses her career. She takes her classes. She selects her wallpaper. As far as possible, a partner has to be free to find out what he or she is like.

We have a close friend who enjoys country music. He has a collection of old Hank Williams records which proves he is hopelessly addicted.

He married a young lady who has been well trained in classical music. She not only appreciates the sound but understands the patterns and movements.

Can the two ever live together? They get along great. She lets him breathe. She doesn't make fun of his music, nor does she try to convert him to European strings.

Insistence to knuckle under is a love killer.

Creative breathing is a far cry from competitiveness. She pursues her interest to gain personal fulfillment. Hopefully, he does the same thing. Only fools try to beat each other. Marriage at its best is complimentary and not competitive.

By the time I met one couple they were well on their way to becoming divorced. They owned a paint and paper store but were not working well together. Finally he decided to open a similar store in a nearby town, to be managed by his wife. The reasoning was that they could buy in greater volume and business would double.

That was the reasoning on the surface. Each evening their conversations seemed to take an ugly turn. They compared each day's sales with glee and despair. The husband couldn't stand to have his wife outsell him. If a customer complained or returned something, the other partner acted like a gold medal finalist.

Within a few months they decided to no longer live together.

When both partners have careers, the competition can be terrific. Especially if she is making more money than he. Many husbands are not ready to handle this one yet. But we are beginning to grow up.

Watch yourselves even now when you play games. Do you have to win? Does your partner take it personally if he loses? This could be a good time to talk it over. Little things are too often icebergs.

When we first got married my wife and I played a game of checkers. Not far into the game I made a triple jump. Pat quit immediately. We have played a lot of games during the past seventeen years but we have yet to play a second game of checkers.

We get along too well to fight over a red and black board. Two strangers are still having the fun of getting to know each other.

6

A GREAT MARRIAGE

That is what your marriage promises to be. One fantastic union.

If we discuss problems too much, we could lose sight of the pleasure. Your marriage has tremendous prospects. It will do you good to stop and recount the great things the two of you have going.

Do you ever wonder why God put marriages together? There are five strong reasons for a good union. If you eventually have all of them going, your relationship will be as healthy as Bruce Jenner with a suntan.

Many partners are extremely happy with only two or three of the five. However, the more of the five you have, the better off you could be. The five are like nails. You can nail a board down with one nail. Through wear and tear the board could break loose after a time. If you have three, four, or five nails there is less likelihood it can move.

Count your nails. You may have more than five. The more you have, the better.

The first nail is the need to complement each other (Gen. 2:18). In short, it means the two of you are pulling together rather than apart. Don't make it more complicated than this.

You can marry someone with a similar personality or an opposite one. One of you can be the wage earner or you both can work.

In the past we have put too much emphasis on the man. We acted as if the woman existed to complement her husband, but not the reverse. Now we admit we know better. A male's role in marriage is to complement his wife (Eph. 5:25).

If you are engaged you probably have little difficulty with this. You come together fairly smoothly, like the fingers on a hand. Sometimes a finger gets out of joint, but generally it is a nice fit. You are going to have a great marriage because you do not work against each other.

The second nail is emotional love. The two of you support each other by tenderly caring (1 Cor. 13).

You have found someone who listens and tries to understand. When something goes great at work you can hardly wait to tell someone. It means all the more if that person really cares what happens to you. At 5:00 you hurry home with a sheepish grin. Sometimes you blurt it out, other times you play it coy. Once in a while you bring a box of candy.

There is something fantastic to share and you have a loving partner who will beam at the news.

When part of your world caves in, there is a shoulder at home and a patient ear. This applies not only to the big ups and downs, but to everything in between. A new tie and a cut finger. A new car and a leaking roof. This is the emotional love most of us need.

You can see it in high gear while you are engaged. Cultivate it. Keep it fresh.

A third nail is physical love (1 Cor. 7:3-5). Sex is a pyramid of strong and varied stones. It is much more than physical release.

Sex is communication. It is a reduction of tension. Sex is simple pleasure. It is a reassurance of belonging.

As an engaged couple, you are moving steadily to its consummation in God's ideal setting—a marriage context. Because your attitudes are healthy, wholesome, and enthusiastic, you will drive this nail deeply.

The fourth nail is having children (Gen. 1:28; Psa. 127:5). Under most conditions, marriage functions as a triangle. Each partner supplies love to the other. They in turn pour out their love in a third direction. Then love travels from the third direction back toward the parents.

Children are not necessary at all times for all couples. However, most partners will find parenthood a fulfilling relationship.

Since both of you have an open attitude toward children, your future looks all the stronger. You can work out the details later.

Adoption will supply this nail just as well as physical birth.

The fifth nail is worship by union (Titus 2:5). This is more than worshiping God together. It is more than going to church.

When our marriage is a loving unit, that relationship is itself a worship to God. People will see your love for each other. They will see the stability of your union. God is pleased when he sees this good use of his institution.

A good marriage is a present to God. When he sees two partners madly in love, he is pleased. When he sees children being raised in wholesomeness, he is gratified.

People see a healthy marriage and they too are made happier. If they know that home is Christian they also receive a favorable witness to the effectiveness of Jesus Christ.

Your great marriage is an offering going up to God. It is acceptable and pleasing to him.

These are only five nails. There are probably more. Maybe you can come up with ten. I would encourage you to try. There are definitely five, and because these are part of your plans, your marriage will be especially strong.

Some marriages do not have all five and the couples are as happy as raccoons at a picnic. Maybe they have decided not to have children. Possibly after some years they have practically given up sex. They have other interests and seldom consider it worth the effort.

Don't assume these marriages are unhappy. They may be getting along excellently on three nails. However, they are the exception. Most couples need every nail they can get. When the wind blows and the rain pours and the house rocks, you will be glad for every solid nail you have. Your marriage will be fantastic because you will carefully drive each nail firm and straight.

But there are more reasons than this for exhilaration. Take time and recount your strengths and weaknesses. Be specific. Talk to your partner about this. What will make this a great marriage? It will help you to write them down.

At first couples are usually too modest to open up, but once you get started, it can flow. This can be a giant step toward feeling re-assured about your marriage.

John started out slowly. Finally he said, "June is so easy to talk to. All day I talk about work or football or even politics. When I see her that evening I can tell her how I really feel. She listens to what is important to me."

Fantastic! It is common strengths that will make this marriage stronger than steel.

Now it's June's turn. "We like to do things together. I've dated some other guys and they always wanted to go places I didn't particularly enjoy. With John it's different."

John comes back. "I enjoy boating and so does June. In good weather we take my boat to the lake."

It isn't that difficult once you get started. We rehearse the problems of marriage. We are flooded with warnings. It is more important to remember all those outstanding qualities you have going.

Take another productive step. Each of you share what you like best about your partner. Why in the world do you love him? Love has reasons.

One young man told me, "Colleen isn't too smart and neither am I, so I figure we will get along great."

Sound the alarm. Abandon ship. What a miserable foundation for a marriage!

By reminding your partner of the features you like most, you reinforce them. Years ago my wife said she really appreciated the way I pick up my own clothes. To this day it haunts me. Every time I start to leave socks on the floor, her compliment echoes in my brain. By pointing out a strength, she made it stronger.

You can do this dozens of times. Do you think she is a neat dresser? Tell her so and you might seal it forever. Do you like her trim figure? Say so and she is more likely to keep it. Say you like her few extra pounds and it will probably have the same effect.

Do you like the way he drives the car? Nail it down before it gets away.

Is he saying "please" and "thank you"? Tell him he is one of the most courteous people you know. He'll eat it up.

Once you start building and reinforcing each other, ask yourselves what your hopes are as a couple. How do you picture yourselves ten years from now? Dream out loud.

Where will your career be? This is not just a question for professional people, but for all with careers. It is a question for both men and women. Does she plan to work? How long? Does she dream of being the manager of a savings and loan? Discuss it now and begin to mesh your dreams together.

Is there a special place you would like to live a few years from now? Do you plan to buy a home? What kind? How will you go about getting a down payment or financing it? It's all hope material.

Discussing dreams openly helps make your sights realistic. It also helps to keep you both on the same track.

What do you like to do together? Be specific. Do you go skating, hiking, bowling, listen to music, play games, work in the church? This will help you see what a wide base of interests you share. If it's only one or two you will want to work at expanding the list. Some marriages suffer from too few interests.

What are your emotional strengths? Pam said, "We get along great until Rich has a problem. Then he clams up and won't talk. He isn't mean, but I wish he would say something."

You don't want to have a stroke every time you get a hangnail, but neither do you want to go into a trance. Solid sharing often does not come easily. While you are engaged, practice working out your emotions in a balanced way.

Some always demand attention. They think what they have to say is the most important. Everything should stop immediately. They interrupt conversations, activities, even phone calls. Listen to what I have to say.

One of my children did this constantly. She was only eight at the time. She still likes to share, but she has more self-control.

We may not always be able to control our emotions but we can work at improving them. Look at the ways you are progressing emotionally. It's a good sign. You feel more comfortable together. Are you managing depression better? Is discouragement becoming less habitual? You are leveling off to a solid, livable pace.

How do you rate your ability to change? If you are becoming more like your partner, don't despair. In most cases this is excellent. If your partner is also becoming like you, the situation is ideal.

Be glad you are not cemented. If one of you were standing still you would have reason for concern. Some partners believe the aim of marriage is for the other partner to conform. Such a person is like a park statue. He never changes himself, except to discolor.

If you can name some positive changes you have made because of your partner, your relationship is throbbing. Keep on exercising. Your goal is not identical twins but compatibility.

Check out your mind growth too. It is an excellent sign to see you reading this book. It is an excellent sign to know you read any books. Relationships can grow from fresh and stimulating ideas—not just about marriage but on practically any subject.

Read the paper, watch the news. You can share and grow by the injection of new material.

While you are discussing good questions, throw this one on the fire. How would you like to improve your partner? Here's a good chance to make progress.

Have you wanted him to give up smoking? Do both of you a favor and let him know now. Most partners are patient and pliable this close to marriage. Be frank but kind.

One partner answered this by saying, "My only wish is that Dave would quit drinking. He doesn't drink much but I can't stand to have it in the house."

We discussed her feelings. Dave had never been drunk and found it hard to understand why she felt so strongly. They could resolve their difference far easier now than they might after marriage. In this case it was no big deal with Dave, and the drinking was gone.

Often the suggestions are appreciated. They know you really love them and only have their interest at heart.

Turn the question around. How could you improve yourself to best help your marriage? There is no need for excessive introspection. Just a quick survey should come up with a couple of winners.

A few solid sacrifices for your partner will be a terrific investment in your marriage. Volunteer without being asked.

You know she thinks the radio is too loud in the car. Next time have it on low and surprise her. She never will get used to your sardines and onions. Switch to tuna fish.

Don't feel like a martyr. It is all part of putting a stable marriage together. And yours really will be a great one.

THE "HIDDEN"
PROBLEM

Lori and Mike were one of the nicest couples you could hope to meet. They had known each other for eighteen months and had been engaged for six. You could tell they were in love, not because they pored over each other but because both glowed like warm ovens.

One of the questions I try to ask a couple is, "How would you change your partner?" After some polite denials, most of them come across with helpful suggestions.

Mike finally pushed it out slowly like toothpaste.

"I wish she wasn't so jealous."

"How is Lori jealous, Mike?" I asked.

"If she sees me even wave at a girl, she won't talk to me. I'm afraid after we are married I won't have any old friends."

"Why?" I wanted to know.

After some discussion the facts became obvious to all three of us. Lori felt she had nothing to offer. She didn't consider herself attractive or capable and only barely likable. Consequently every situation was a threat to her.

Lori represents millions of people who have little respect for themselves. Their inability to let go and love themselves can cause great strain on their marriage.

If there is only one present you can give to your partner, make it a healthy respect for yourself. It is much easier to love someone who has a healthy love for himself.

For years I counseled husbands and wives who had "little" problems. They complained about money, sex, and communication. One day after a frustrating session I sat back bewildered. For an hour I had discussed a "silly" situation with a young married lady. Finally we applied a bandage and she left with a sense of relief. But it was only one of many problems she had. Then it dawned on me. This woman has so little respect for herself that she will always be swamped with small problems. If she is ever to level off, she must adopt a healthy love for herself.

A young lady wrote and described her husband. She loved him enormously. In her list of attributes Jan wrote, "Jim has a good love for himself."

She didn't resent this. Jan was smart enough to know this worked for the good of everybody. Jim did not have to be continuously babied. He had too much respect for himself. Jim wouldn't abandon his family to go out and "seek his manhood." He was too secure for that.

Jan had reason to thank God. She had found a man who loved himself. I think Jim was just as fortunate.

For some of us this idea will take some getting used to. We are often taught that self-respect is selfishness. This isn't the case at all. The *lack* of self-love leads to selfishness. The person who has to be the center of attention is seeking love. The individual who must hoard everything is never satisfied with himself.

Jesus Christ told us to love our neighbor as ourself (Matt. 19:19). The love of myself is what sets me free to love other people. Self-defacing limits us. Self-love does not equal selfishness. Self-doubt often does.

Everyone should meet Erv. He would do anything for you. Not just if you asked him; he would look for ways to help, regardless. Erv loves himself. He took flying lessons, went to graduate school part-time, went hunting, sang in a quartet. He was the busiest person you could imagine, yet he was the most unselfish man. Self-love and selfishness do not have to be the same thing.

If we don't consider ourselves lovable, we will make it tough on our partners.

Deep inside, most of us probably do love ourselves. Many of us are embarrassed by it. We don't know how to handle it. Often we have been taught it is wrong. We spend much of our lives trying to smother it. Now we need to accept a balanced concept. The Bible tells us it is OK to love ourself because it leads to a love for others.

"My husband doesn't love me." She was a young, attractive redhead with despair in her voice. "I didn't believe he loved me when we were going together, and after three years of marriage I still don't believe it."

Her cry for help was the same one raised by thousands of other married people. Her husband was considerate, thoughtful, and careful to tell her how much he loved her. Still something inside kept telling her he didn't. She simply didn't love herself.

The Apostle Paul understood this principle. He wrote to tell husbands to love their wives as they love themselves (Eph. 5:28).

Before you stand at the altar, do your partner a gigantic favor. Sit down and make a list of all the things you do well. Little things you never think of. Big things you do all the time. Don't stop until you have ten. If you can give twenty, you are really sailing.

Many will find this hard to do. A few will never get it done. It is an attempt to look at yourself realistically rather than surrendering to the great put-down. Do anything you care to with the note. Maybe you will want to give it to your partner and explain it. Possibly you will want to trade lists. Whether your mate ever sees it or not isn't what counts. The fact that you made it will be the greatest wedding present you could give.

Not only do you need this opinion of yourself, you need to keep it. Many couples start their marriage feeling great and soon go under. With children to feed, floors to scrub, and a career to pursue, it is easy to come apart. Our marriages can't afford that.

There is presently a commercial on television advertising a tonic. A married couple look at each other and say, "We take good care of ourselves." The advertisement is a bit hard to watch and I don't know if the product works. I do know the principle is sound.

Fatigue and pressure are termites to any marriage. They will destroy your concept of yourself. Promise yourself you will help your marriage by keeping yourself in good condition physically, mentally, and spiritually.

The way we feel about ourselves is contagious. If we consider ourselves worthless we will pass it on to our children. Our feelings of uselessness will eventually affect our mate, both directly and indirectly.

Paul teaches that a man should accept his wife as part of his body and give her the same love and care he would give himself. A sane man does not cut off his hand or intentionally run a tractor over his foot.

If a person considers himself unworthy, useless, or friendless, he may transfer that feeling to his wife. His thinking may go something like this: I do not deserve good food, consequently we do not deserve good food. I do not like having friends over, consequently we do not have friends over. I am not capable of being a leader, therefore I am embarrassed when my wife leads.

Ephesians 5:28 spells out what is essential to a balanced marriage. Take a happy, healthy attitude toward your spouse in the same way you take a happy, healthy attitude toward yourself.

A wife complains to a counselor: "He never talks to me. He won't give me his opinion or take any leadership. What am I supposed to do?" That problem gets listed as a communication breakdown. In reality the husband is unsure of himself, does not think his opinion is worthwhile, and would rather remain silent than sound foolish. He actually has a problem of low self-esteem. The refusal to communicate is only the symptom of the difficulty and not the cause.

Jane was in her mid-twenties and had been married five years. She found it impossible to enjoy sex.

"I wish he would leave me alone. It just gives me the creeps to know he is coming after me. In the daytime everything is fine, but I dread nighttime."

It sounds like a classic sex problem. Where is the root cause? Is he an offensive or clumsy lover? Maybe she had a bad experience in her youth.

After talking to Jane for two sessions, the difficulty became apparent to both of us. She thought of herself as ugly. She couldn't imagine anyone wanting to make love to her. Her entire body would go frigid just to think of the encounter. Rather than flooding her with sex literature I began to deal with the "hidden" problem.

Couples who are deeply in love could be heading for critical conflicts without understanding the reason. We need to back off and ask crucial questions about our self-esteem.

Fortunately there is help available for just such a difficulty. We need to accept some simple but startling facts about ourselves. Here are some things we need to tell ourselves and rehearse often.

I am a valuable person. Sometimes, standing nose deep in self-pity, we tell ourselves we don't amount to anything. We consider ourselves "Mr. Zero," the dandruff of the world. This false modesty sounds pious among Christians. However, the Bible won't let us get away with it. God created us in his image (Gen. 1:27) and, as we know, man fell and lost some of that image (Rom. 5:12). But if this is all we know, we have heard only part of the good news. Jesus Christ picked us up, dusted us off, and reunited us with God (Col. 1:21, 22).

No longer a ding-a-ling, man has a purpose and plan in life. God considers people valuable for his program in this world.

A despondent wife sits on the sofa engulfed in a cloud of gloom. She feels useless. She is not any good. Her children would be better off without her. You can combat this scene by placing some simple facts in order and keeping them there. God considers us so valuable he has placed us in his special family.

I am capable. It is difficult for many people to admit they can do anything. I have asked individuals to make a list of ten things they do well. They have agonized, sweated, and strained over it. Finally they came back and said, "Forget it." They simply couldn't force themselves to do it.

To say we are capable sounds like pride, conceit, and all those other nasty things. For many it is a mental hurdle they cannot leap.

In the marriage relationship this feeling burns like the hot sun through a glass. He hates to fix anything, so she assumes he is lazy. Quite the contrary; he thinks he is incapable of fixing anything. She doesn't want to try anything new. He thinks she is an old-fashioned stick-in-the-mud. The fact is, she doesn't think she can do anything new or she will fail.

Romans 12:3-8 tells us to not think of ourselves more highly than we ought. It seems everyone knows that part. What many fail to realize is that this passage goes on to say that people should have a sober judgment or face the facts. The facts are that believers have gifts that God gave them, which they need to recognize and use. To feel that one can do nothing is a denial of reality.

You are a gifted person. I don't have to know you or give a battery of tests. The fact that you are a person means you are gifted. Celebrate that giftedness rather than deny it.

I am loved. A baseball player for the Kansas City Royals got into a fight with New York Yankee players. A reporter later said to him, "You know the Yankees are really mad at you." He replied,

"I have a wife and two children who love me. I don't need to have the Yankees love me too."

Great wisdom! Too many people want everyone to love them. Because not everyone loves them, they assume no one does. A case of tragic extremes.

"I was married five years before I believed she loved me." That is a sad statement because the husband's feelings have robbed him of a great deal of happiness. However, this is not an uncommon feeling. Yet this is usually all it is, just a feeling.

Do your mate a huge favor. Resolve for yourself once and for all that your partner loves you. Otherwise you will find it difficult to relax and give yourself to your spouse.

It is amazing how many people do not believe anyone loves them. Some Christians do not believe God loves them. Children do not believe their parents love them. Spouses believe no one cares.

Rather than accepting true love, which rises above circumstances, they continue to play an immature game called "Nobody loves me." The result is a very self-centered life. "Where will I find love?" "Is he mad at me?" "She wishes she had never married me."

Some terribly rude things can be said between married couples. A partner often becomes less careful after the honeymoon. That shouldn't frighten us. Couples are also kind and loving. But after months or years of familiarity it becomes easy to be thoughtlessly frank. "Those slacks look crummy." "Didn't we eat this last night?" "You are always watching football." Sometimes these phrases thrown around loosely can cut deeply. They might lead you to wonder if you are really loved.

Drive this nail firmly and you can depend on it. True love is not a magic act—now you see it, now you don't. A few thoughtless statements and careless actions cannot erase your love for each other. You are loved and you can count on it.

Because some people are always seeking love and never finding it, they have trouble leading a balanced life. They find it difficult to relax and even more difficult to help others.

You are correct. You are not the most loved person in the world. Neither are you the most hated. You are you. You have someone who is willing to spend the rest of his life with you. You are greatly loved.

Certainly God doesn't love his children with a fickle love. Jeremiah said, "For long ago the Lord had said to Israel: I have loved you, O my people, with an everlasting love; with lovingkindness I have drawn you to me" (31:3).

God's love is constant and unchanging. Most of us will have a mate who is basically the same way. Some only imagine their spouses change like a kaleidoscope with each flick of the wrist. Most likely a partner has contributed plenty to prove love. The next time they say it—we should just believe it.

I am improving. "We have been married for fifteen years and we love each other more today than we did then."

Do you ever wonder how many say this and don't really mean it? I think some are just pretending. You have to say something and you can't say, "This marriage is lousy." Yet others mean it with a deep and warm conviction.

What is the difference between the sincere ones and the put-ons? Which one will you be a dozen years from now? Just possibly the "why" is because they have grown and improved during their years together.

"I wouldn't go back to dating for anything." The man who said this had been married for years. "The uncertainty, the anxiety. It seemed like fun then but it doesn't rate compared to the dependability of marriage."

They know, they share, they trust, they confide much more than they ever did before. They have matured and accept each other more. Their life together really is richer.

Many people have trouble finding the comfortable middle in life. They wrestle continuously between inferiority and superiority. Today he thinks he is the greatest and his ego lifts like steam whistling out of a kettle. The next day he is the world's worst and tries to join the night crawlers under a damp rock.

After years of war within yourself you finally admit the facts. "I am not inferior. I am not superior. I am me." You have grown and improved and your family will be better off for it.

But this shouldn't surprise us. Paul wrote, "And I am sure that God who began the good work within you will keep right on helping you grow in his grace until his task within you is finally finished on that day when Jesus Christ returns" (Phil. 1:6).

Does this promise apply just to missionaries or new Christians? It applies to people, and people make up marriages. Because people are improving, your marriage will improve also.

If God wills I will live tomorrow, you can improve and both partners can thank God for that.

It is reasonable to love myself. Most men are not the best husbands in the world, but neither are they the worst. They are just good husbands. They will look back at terrible blunders they made. Sometimes they really embarrassed their wives. Many husbands will also remember the things they did that brought the broadest smile and brightest sparkle ever to light up a wife.

There are times when husbands or wives have done the job well. It would do us good to admit it to ourselves. It will even encourage us to do well the next time

I find it easier to emphasize the negative. I can remember failures in living, vivid color. It would be hard to forget them since I recite them over and over again.

A few years ago I took a step toward combating this negativism. Now I collect and keep every compliment I get. If I get a thank-you note or letter I no longer throw it away. I keep them in a special drawer. Every once in a while I take them out and go over them. It's a great morale builder.

I look at those notes and say to myself, "Yes, I did that. This was fun. I'm proud of that job." Sometimes it helps keep me in balance.

Rehearse the things you do well. It can help you do even better next time.

God reminds us it is good to have a healthy love for ourselves. It is out of this health that we will best be able to love others and especially our partners.

"That is how husbands should treat their wives, loving them as parts of themselves. For since a man and his wife are now one, a man is really doing himself a favor and loving himself when he loves his wife" (Eph. 5:28).

If self-love, self-respect, self-worth can all be handled in correct proportion, the net result is freedom. Freedom for yourself, your partner, and eventually your family. It is all right if your husband goes hunting because you like to go bowling. Your husband is free to pursue a career because you have some goals you want to accomplish.

The two of you are not jealous—you are not in competition. Consequently, you are not afraid to let go. You realize you can better keep someone by giving him freedom.

In the past some fathers or mothers have smothered their families.

They wanted everyone close each evening. They insisted the household revolve around them. Often they were trying to manipulate a love which they did not have for themselves.

You are free. Free to commit yourselves to each other. Not because your partner demands allegiance but because you want to give. Because you are happy with yourself you are not afraid to give yourself to someone else.

8

SEXUAL LIMBO

Engagement is the birth of enormous sexual frustration and hope. The two of you want each other. Nothing could be more natural. If you have no sex drive, there is reason to see a doctor. If you don't find each other appealing, you might as well call it off.

The feelings you have are healthy and God-given. If we weren't sex magnets, the population would soon dwindle. We would also miss a great deal of happiness.

Now that you are "promised" to each other, the desire will probably intensify. Congratulations! Everything is going according to schedule.

The problem is, you sort of "half" own each other. You fully intend to marry. Only weeks or months stand between you and sexual fulfillment. The question now is whether you will hold off until marriage and enjoy sex in its fullest freedom.

It has to be an uneasy problem. Statistics tell us many couples are participating in premarital, extramarital, and nonmarital sex. At present television seems to be promoting sex outside of a marriage context. Most situation comedies feature characters who are not married.

Does it make any sense for a young couple to wait until they are married? Our society is increasingly tolerant of premarital sex. It is often treated as not only acceptable but cute.

Frankly, engaged couples can do what they want today. If they are adult enough to marry, they should be mature enough to intelligently decide about their sex life. However, the fact that they have this freedom doesn't mean they have to use it.

I am free to bake in the sun for hours and burn like bacon. But I don't have to do it to prove I am free. I am at liberty to throw my money down a sewer grate—another freedom I choose to ignore.

Anyone who chooses premarital sex and doesn't care about the consequences probably isn't mature enough to marry.

With so many opinions and practices being freely publicized, young people will have to make up their own minds. Whose system of ethics and conduct are they willing to accept?

Fortunately, the Bible offers direct guidance on the subject. It is a book of understanding and practical instruction. God knows how you feel right now. He appreciates your dreams, hopes, desires, and frustrations.

Knowing exactly what we are going through, God tells us to stay away from premarital intercourse. "That is why I say to run from sex sin. No other sin affects the body as this one does. When you sin this sin it is against your own body" (1 Cor. 6:18).

Jesus Christ reminded us again that physical union is marriage union. "The two shall become one—no longer two, but one! And no man may divorce what God has joined together" (Matt. 19:6).

Sexual fads and practices come and go. One day it is popular, even fashionable, to entertain sexual adventures. Trial marriages and living together become daring. However, tomorrow the wind shifts and we are off chasing the next illusion.

We need a dependable guideline. God unflinchingly offers us one.

In our enlightened age we might think the traditional warnings are no longer necessary. With birth control the risk of premature pregnancy should be gone. With massive education the threat of venereal disease should be eliminated. Yet in some American cities the number of abortions exceeds the number of regular births. V.D. is at an all-time high.

These facts seem almost too obvious to mention. They sound like old scare tactics which won't work in a modern society. Yet it is embarrassing to see how widespread these consequences are. Premarital sex remains both physically unsafe and unwise.

We are suspicious that these are not the ultimate reasons for God's warning. They are important, but only by-products. The essential reason for waiting has to do with the marriage relationship.

Sex is a special form of communication you save for one person.

It comforts, it relaxes, reassures, and sometimes makes you want to shout. It is reserved by both the male and female for one person who needs the ultimate communication. God considers it too majestic to share indiscriminately.

Smart partners will make up their minds early. There are many couples who wish they had waited until marriage. I have never met a Christian couple who were sorry they waited.

When you have made your commitment to wait, there are several steps you need to consider. They are practical and unspectacular You can add some suggestions of your own.

Couples need to avoid bumming around. After they have gone together for a while, it becomes easier to sit around and do nothing in particular. Often these nothing dates degenerate quickly. The young people begin to kiss or pet partly out of boredom. Frankly, they have nothing else to do with their hands. There is no plan to get heavy, but there is really nothing better to do. Couples may find themselves far more involved than they expected to be.

It is important to plan your evening. Develop some mutual interests and activities. These will prove beneficial when you are married.

A wise person once told a group of young people to "get out of those cars." They laughed at him. How prudish can you be? When they grew up they told their children, "Get out of those cars." Their children laughed at them.

And so the generations go. Two people parked in a car are a certain invitation for sexual adventure. All of us know it is true. When you are young you hate to admit it.

The person who really wants to avoid premarital intercourse will stay away from places where it is likely to happen. If you want to save money you stay out of stores. When you want to wait until marriage, you avoid traps.

Certain movies must put intense pressure on couples. You have the right to attend. However, only the foolish think they can handle everything.

No engaged couple can afford to ignore Hamburg's law. Briefly stated, it says a couple never regresses physically. If a couple kisses, they will kiss again. If they fondle, they will fondle again. If they have intercourse, they will again.

The partners who say, "Let's do it just once" are kidding themselves. Couples do not regress in physical love. They either repeat or progress. They seldom quit.

71

Maybe you are the exception. Most people think they are. They find out too late they are not. Guard your physical progress or it will soon get out of control.

It is easy to see why a young person is in a physical "rush." He has rounded the corner of twenty and by now has survived strong sexual pressure. Magazines, literature, jokes, films have all painted the real and the supposed glories of sex. His own body has ached for sexual release. How much longer does he have to wait? He has found the person he wants to marry. Both partners imagine that sexual adventure can only strengthen their relationship.

Don't let your physical needs fog your brain. Intercourse may only complicate your needs rather than ease your tension. Surveys indicate a third to a half of all engagements break up. Your marriage may not be as definite as you hope. Frequently the frustrations accompanying premarital sex lead to an eventual split.

Many young people argue late into the night over how much difference a piece of paper makes. If they are married in their hearts, can't they also be married with their bodies?

It is true, a biblical definition of marriage is two people joining in sexual love. Isaac is a good example. He married Rebekah by taking her to his tent. Jacob evidently married Rachel by sleeping with her (Gen. 24:67; 29:30). Two people became one flesh.

However, God has given government the right to regulate marriage. If the law asks for a certificate, the Christian is happy to comply. Even if the laws should change, Christian marriage will remain a total commitment.

Arguments against the government's rights are mere contortions. They are irrational attempts to sidestep the law in order to surrender to lust.

When a couple starts to give in to this illogic, they need to stop and ask themselves some questions. Just what is the hurry? Why not get a piece of paper? Is this an indication of the impetuous behavior which will mark the marriage? Are you sure both of you are mature enough to handle these important decisions? Just being in a hurry is no sign you are ready to marry.

Marriage is filled with little surprises. You will want to start it with the most solid foundations possible. Patience will pay large dividends later.

"But let patience have her perfect work, that ye may be perfect and entire, wanting nothing" (Jas. 1:4, KJV).

As you put a Christian standard to work, there are certain myths which must be erased. There is much nonsense being passed around with no basis in fact.

For instance, the rumor that everyone is doing it is a complete fairy tale. It is the same story which passed around a generation ago. Many couples do participate in premarital intercourse. But millions do not. And yet they could if they wanted to. Movies are particularly devastating in distorting the facts. They often make it appear that every couple is involved in sex. This is far from the case even among college students.

Yet it is an argument that is hard to dismiss. When we get the feeling "everyone" does it, we begin to wonder about ourselves. Are we weird because we haven't? Is there something terrific in youth I might miss? Consequently, the pressure becomes tremendous.

It takes a particularly secure person to resist in the light of these trends. The "pack" person falls easily to this argument. The thinker will stop and decide for himself. The Christian knows there are more important things to consider than trends or surveys.

Another myth which needs exposure is the trial marriage approach. Two are supposed to have sex to see if they are physically compatible. Possibly they won't enjoy each other in bed. Is it better to find out now?

As laudable as this sounds to some, the facts prove the opposite. In their surveys, Dr. Judson Landis and Dr. Evelyn Duvall both found evidence that premarital sex is unprofitable. Most women seldom experienced sexual climax with intercourse before marriage. However, the frequency rose considerably after the two adapted during marriage.

Before marriage the couple has sex without commitment. Tomorrow the relationship could end. They hold a promise to each other but both realize it is not binding. Should they fail to enjoy this they could merely elect to split.

There is no such thing as laboratory marriage. We are not white mice. There can be no experiments in this field. Two people cannot pretend to care and pretend total commitment and get the same result.

The smart couple will learn a number of things about each other before marriage. Sex performance and compatibility are not among them. Most couples adapt and improve their sex experience because they are dedicated to success, not because they are experimenting.

Too many couples are still engaging in premarital sex to "prove" they love their partner. It is as old as stone. Before you slide easily into this pattern, face some facts.

The partner who demands sex as proof of love is flatly exploitative. He is looking out for himself at your expense. How you feel about it is not his primary concern. He has an ego to satisfy. It is much like deer hunting, and you are the deer. He needs to score in order to please himself. If a partner continues to act this way, he is sending a clear message. The individual is extremely selfish and generally will be looking out for himself. How you might be used or your feelings hurt is not his major interest.

Do yourself a favor and think this person over. The rest of your life may be spent as the servant of a tireless tyrant. At least you need to discuss this matter and reach some satisfaction.

On the other hand, what type of person feels the need to give in to such selfishness? If you want to wait until marriage but give in beforehand, what kind of strength are you showing? If you feel so insecure that you cannot hold your ground, how will you fare after marriage? Can it survive with one dominant figure demanding your compliance?

Of course, you think, it will be different when you get married. The two of you won't have these frustrations and you can join in gladly. Don't kid yourself. The patterns you set in engagement are often the same ones that linger through a lifetime.

God is far from being opposed to sex. He only wants it practiced under healthy control. This is why he made it a pleasure rather than a pain. Far from being against it, God is the promoter of married sex (1 Cor. 7:1-5).

There are good reasons for lines down the middle of highways. Waterways may be open, but careful laws keep them safe.

"If a godly man compromises with the wicked, it is like polluting a fountain or muddying a spring" (Prov. 25:26).

Despite the strong teaching of the Scriptures there are many who have had premarital intercourse. Unfortunately too many of these never feel forgiven and free from their sin. If the Bible is to be presented completely it cannot be merely a warning against premarital intercourse. After someone has broken the law, the grace of God will then forgive and restore the person fully.

"He never bears a grudge, nor remains angry forever. He has not punished us as we deserve for all our sins, for his mercy toward those who fear and honor him is as great as the height of the heavens above the earth. He has removed our sins as far away from us as the east is from the west. He is like a father to us, tender and sympathetic to those who reverence him" (Psa. 103:9-13).

Have you already had premarital intercourse? There is no need to continue to drag this guilt around. God promises to forgive those who in true repentance ask his forgiveness.

The person who has had sex before marriage is wrong. God doesn't equivocate. But it would be hypocritical for the rest of us to judge that person harshly. "Yes, all have sinned; all fall short of God's glorious ideal; yet now God declares us 'not guilty' of offending him if we trust in Jesus Christ, who in his kindness freely takes away our sins" (Rom. 3:23).

No matter how far you go physically, the engagement period is trying. You love the person you are committed to. The person is attractive, appealing, and interesting. Marriage will mean the two of you will sleep together and enjoy sex. You can't be considered odd if you want to hurry that up.

If you have had intercourse, don't think the marriage can't work. Thousands of couples who have had premarital sex go on to highly successful marriages. However, many of them need to take time to deal with what has happened. They are better off because they have aired it and cleared their feelings. And ultimate healing is possible only because of genuine repentance, confession to God and restoration.

Communicate with each other during the engagement period. Tell your partner how you feel about sex. Then plan together what you can do to keep it in bounds until the right time comes.

9

LOVE
COMMUNICATES

When she put on her shoe, her toes felt funny. She reached inside and found a piece of white paper. Written in red ink were the simple words: "I love you today." It wasn't signed and it didn't have to be. She had the greatest husband in the world. For the rest of the day the young lady would have her battery charged. Her husband had communicated without saying a word out loud.

Most engaged couples seem to find it easy to communicate. They have so much to talk about. There are plans to make, futures to dream, and new frontiers to explore in each other's personality.

Not only are there reasons to communicate, there are also many avenues. An engaged couple can look into each other's eyes and talk for fifteen minutes without saying a word. A hand placed on hers says more than hours of conversation.

The key to a lasting love is to keep it this way. The smart couple will have open, flowing lines to make it easy to say all the things which need to be said.

Barbara and Don used to go for long walks before they were married. But after the rings are put in place, life has a way of becoming complicated. He had to finish graduate school, and then, of course, there was the career he had to develop. Soon their life started to pull apart rather than melt together.

In the process they forgot the little things. They were too busy to take walks anymore. Everything was hurried and fast cars were the only way to move. They were too busy to sit and drink from each other's eyes. Love itself had to be hurried and hectic.

Married life doesn't have to be this way. A happy couple can take the communication they have as engaged youth and build on it. Don't give up the little things you have now, but keep adding new and exciting avenues.

To some of us the word communication sounds so official and heavy. Like an official "summit." If things are going badly or something drastic is about to happen, we had better stop and communicate. Maybe we had best make an appointment.

There are some summits in marriage, but not many. There are less critical conversations for those who keep in touch along the way.

It was hard to imagine we would ever stop talking. When we walked around Washington, D.C., sat in little restaurants, or called each other, there was so much to say. It was all new, interesting, and exciting.

After you are married it becomes easy to hide behind a newspaper or dissolve into work. It is sometimes a long time before something new happens. We have discussed each other's relatives several times and there is little new to say. Some family counselors say 80 percent of those who come to see them have the same complaint—"We can't seem to talk to each other."

One day I was standing in my kitchen with a friend. He picked up a note off the table and read it. The note said, "You are a great love, Pat." My friend looked at me, smiled the world's most devilish grin, and said, "It must be nice."

I was embarrassed. But he was right! It was nice.

Some of the best advice I received before marriage came from a patent lawyer. He said, "After you get married, keep doing the little things." Instead of buying the big gift once a year, why not a long-stemmed rose every couple of weeks? Instead of the $6.00 box of candy, try one for fifty-nine cents. The little frequent reminders are the things that turn a heart to putty.

A middle-aged man once explained why he called his wife every night when he was on the road. His first wife had died and it had devastated his heart. Never again could he take his wife for granted. Every night he was determined to communicate just a little.

"She never says anything," was Russell's complaint. "I'm the kind of guy who enjoys talking—but it really gets to me when she just hangs on."

Not an uncommon statement. Sometimes the girl is the talker and the guy is Calvin Coolidge. It would be surprising to find a couple who both enjoyed talking and listening in exact proportion.

After all, marriage is an adjustment. A happy adjustment, hopefully, but an adjustment nevertheless. Both partners need to move toward the center. Russell needs to talk less and his lady needs to talk more. That is no problem. The problem arises when one partner assumes that his rate of communication is the ideal. Then he can't understand why his mate doesn't become like him. That attitude is trouble.

This is part of the reason why sex is so important. It is not just that there is need for physical release, and not just that sex is fun (and it is that). Rather, if sex had no other function, it is a great help as simple communication.

Sex in a married context says "I love you." It says someone cares. When things get cold and harsh outside, close, warm physical contact is a message. Sex is love at a high plateau when it indicates someone cares.

Whatever the form of communication, it has to avoid the extremes. On the one end there are the door crashers. At the other end are the silent nodders.

The door crasher is the impatient type. He wants to talk about everything *right now*. "Let's get it out in the open," is his motto. He has a dangerous attitude. Some things need to settle. They need time to mellow and age. Often these will take care of themselves.

Forcing issues too hard and fast just might cause them to break. The sensitive mate learns to read his partner. He knows when to rush in and when to wait in the wings.

Sometimes we get hurt and are hurt learning the difference. But it's worth it to find out.

Smiling nodders are just as bad. They don't feel the need to say anything. They merely grin and assume everything will be all right. Nonsense. No one—absolutely no one—likes to be taken for granted. Anyone who only needed a silent grinner could have married Mount Rushmore.

Pry yourself loose. Make yourself communicate. If it is small, that may be just the touch. Somehow the message that you care must get across in easy to understand terms.

Most communication isn't by the words we say. Experts in the field tell us only 7 percent of communication is by words. Inflection and tone make up 38 percent. Facial expression delivers the other 55 percent.

If you doubt this, try an experiment. Practice saying, "Honey, you can do it anyway you like." Say it gleefully. Try it scornfully. Say it defiantly. Give it your angry look and tone.

Words don't mean much. After a big fight, someone will say, "Well, I don't understand. I told him he could go ahead." The important thing is how you told him he could go ahead. You know what it is like to be told you can do something, but understand by the tone that you don't dare.

It is hard to overstate the influence we have over our partner. When the two of you meet at the end of a day that first greeting is terrifically important. "How did the day go, honey?" "The pits," is the acid reply. Those two words have set the tenor.

She would have been better off to have said something good about the day. The news about the dented car could have been saved until after dinner.

The person coming in the door needs the same loving care. A sad face, a grin, a wink can make all the difference.

A man came home one evening after a terrible day. There was no other way to describe it. He piled out of the car with stooped shoulders and a face like a bulldog. Suddenly he stopped himself. "I can't take this inside." He had three children and a hard-working wife. If he crawled inside, the entire atmosphere of the house would drop like a rock. He straightened himself, forced a smile, and marched inside like a conquering hero.

We owe it to the person we love to try and stay on top. *You* are the biggest influence in his or her daily life. Not the only one—just the biggest.

A junior high counselor told me about some role modeling he does in class. He pairs off couples and asks them to pretend they are parents. Almost always they are gruff, loud—practically violent. Seldom are they polite, caring, or affectionate. The reason they do this is because they are self-conscious youth—or is that the reason?

Before we go too far with our communication emphasis, one rule should be kept in mind. Some things aren't worth saying. A man says, "I can say anything I want to my wife." Shame on you.

The Bible says, "A man with good sense holds his tongue" (Prov. 11:12). Everyone needs a filter between his brain and his tongue. We think many things we shouldn't say. We think many things we shouldn't even think.

There is a point at which frankness becomes ugly. The person who always shoots off how he thinks is dangerous. He is going to help a few people. He will hurt many more. If he is smart he will learn to harness it. The Bible says there is a time to keep silence (Eccl. 3:7). Only a fool ignores it (Prov. 10:14).

A wise mate chooses his words carefully. Words are hard to swallow later.

A man was yelling at his wife in haste. Words rolled off his tongue thoughtlessly. Finally he said, "I wish I had never married you." Later he regretted that little outburst. He apologized. They made up. Everything is forgotten. But in the back of her mind those words still shift around.

Maybe the wife has just bought a new dress and she wants to show it to you. It cost $60 and she is waiting for your approval. Your mind tells you, "It looks like a salmon left too long in the sun." She is going to wear it. If you tell her "anything you want," you are acting like an insensitive clod. There is a time to be quiet and kind.

The "let's get it all out in the open" cult can be cruel. It won't hurt to eat a baked potato once a month. It might not kill you to go to the races once in a while. Some things are better done just because you love.

There was a time when I felt the need to always talk. If someone had a problem I had to have an answer. When someone was sick or had died I felt the need to make mini-speeches. Sometimes it is the worst thing we could do.

Some days your partner will need to have you sit and hold his hand. No need to say or promise anything. Your hand in his will say everything.

Part of the happiness of marrying is that you will get to know someone as you have never known anyone—his moods, ups, downs. We don't have to be afraid of that intimate knowledge. Sometimes it's a lot of fun.

As we study each other we find what soars the other person high and what sends her crashing. The smart mate learns to play the other like a finely tuned harp. Without apologies we learn to manipulate in the kindest way.

When is the best time to break good news? What about bad news? You can't keep bad news for very long. But an hour or two could make a tremendous difference. When your partner is weighed down, tired, confused, even depressed, be careful. He doesn't need a millstone dropped in his lap.

Communication at its best is helpful. There are many things to complain about. Inflation is terrible, the children will need shoes, war is always breaking out. Our conversations often have a way of developing a trend. Some of us are always discussing the negative. Everything is bad, rotten, and getting worse. This attitude is contagious. Words like fun, better, interesting, exciting, and grateful are also contagious. If you were in charge of epidemics, what kind would you order?

The Bible has some helpful advice. It tells us to stay away from corrupt communication (Eph. 4:29). All of us can major on the positive and constructive. For some it will take a retraining of our thought patterns. We can do it. We will be tremendously glad we did.

Proverbs 12:18 says, "There is that speaketh like the piercings of a sword: but the tongue of the wise is health" (KJV).

Some morning, say to yourself, "I can help my mate get off to a good day." I'll put a love note in her purse. I can prepare the breakfast he likes best. I'll volunteer to order tickets for the concert.

You can't control the entire day—nor do you want to. But you can go a long mile to give it a great start. *No one* affects your mate as much as you do.

It may seem silly to take lessons on how to talk at your age. You might be surprised at the number of people who can't. Probably the hardest part to conquer is the ability to say, "I'm sorry." Practice it. The smart partner will say it often.

Practice these in front of a mirror:

"I have been stubborn."

"I was wrong."

"That was selfish of me."

"I won't do that again."

"I'm sorry."

These are elementary but good building blocks. The person who can say them sincerely has a great marriage ahead.

Jack was the kind of person who thought he could say "I'm sorry." He and his wife, Bev, were determined to iron things out. When you listen to Jack you can see immediately what his problem was.

"I am sorry I called your sister a witch, but you weren't kind to my brother."

As Jack saw it, he had apologized. What more could she want? This is the way many of us apologize. We use apology as an excuse to

81

attack our partner. There is no sincerity, no sign of contrition. By apologizing we only inflame the situation.

When you say "I'm sorry," speak only about your problem. We are like children trying to hide our fault behind someone else's. Maturity takes responsibility. It learns to say, "I was wrong."

The psalmist said, "I will declare mine iniquity; I will be sorry for my sin" (Psa. 38:18, KJV). Don't drag anyone else into it.

A healthy love will initiate the apology. You may be wasting hours and days waiting for your partner to act first. Whose responsibility is it to apologize? That one's easy. It's *yours.* But you didn't start it. It's still yours. We miss a great deal of love arguing over who started the argument. That is academic. You be the peace maker, and keep your love warm.

Can you remember walking into a house filled with tension? The static is terrible. Be wise and keep it short. One day our oldest daughter said, "I don't know what is wrong, but something is." My wife and I hadn't said a word, but the tension was obvious. We have too much to lose by letting it drag on.

Many couples keep their communications at a high level. It's great to meet two partners who still talk to each other with respect. They kid around and tease, but there is no meanness or callousness. They are polite and honor each other's opinion. They haven't lost their charm. They practice saying "thank you."

One couple says "thank you" as a regular habit. They miss once in a while, but the attitude is there and so are the words. If you could meet their children you would really be impressed. They say "thank you" too—for little things. A ride in the car. When they stop for a coke. Dinner at a restaurant. No one rides over them, they just say it. Their parents establish an atmosphere of charm and it rubs off automatically on the children.

You look at your spouse and say "thanks" for the meal. "I appreciate all the preparations." Those words make fireworks go off in a girl's heart.

You look at your husband and say, "We discuss money a lot but I am grateful. We have a place to live, furniture, a car, braces for the kids' teeth. God has been generous."

Sometimes you will want to sit your mate down and say, "I know your job gets tough. But thanks for doing it for us." Words guaranteed to make a person feel nine feet tall.

The Bible tells us to have our conversation seasoned with salt

(Col. 4:6). If you are ever forced to go on a salt-free diet, this verse will be easy to understand. Food becomes tasteless without salt.

We give our partner communication which has good salt. It's tasteful, helpful, loving.

You take your partner by the hand and sit on the sofa. You tell her she is soft. Tell him he is strong. From there on it is easy. Then you say, "Honey, I love you just because you are you." Now you are communicating.

10
GETTING GOOD
ADVICE

Everybody needs help sometimes. It may be advice on hanging wall-paper or how to get your car fixed. Wise counselors come in handy, even when there are no serious problems.

Maybe you are one of those who has to find out everything for yourself. Life is trial and error for you. I appreciate that spirit. I also know it can lead to a great many knocks and bruises.

A couple came in for premarital counseling even though I wasn't going to marry them. They lived in another state and were going back to her church.

The girl seemed impatient. "I told Roger we might just as well get your opinion too." It was clear that she wanted to be somewhere else.

She had a good point. She was also missing another one. There is no end to collecting opinions. *Too many* counselors are both confusing and counterproductive. Don't keep bouncing questions off every bobbing head you meet.

But look at the other side of that coin. Friendly, open advice can save hours of agony. In more than one case it could have rescued a marriage.

"Plans go wrong with too few counselors; many counselors bring success" (Prov. 15:22).

There is still another way to look at counseling. Unless you hear the guidelines, you don't know which ones to break. Not every piece of advice is golden. Certainly not every one applies to your marriage. But it's good to hear, weigh, sift, and choose.

Before we were married we talked to two people about the practical aspects of living together. The first one was a minister during several sessions of premarital counseling. I didn't like being there for two reasons: first, because we had to be. He would not have married us if we hadn't shown up. Second, the minister did all the talking and I felt preached to.

After we were married a couple of years I changed my mind completely. The minister's advice turned out to be such excellent counseling that it still echoes in my life. He gave us practical suggestions and biblical guidelines. They make more sense all the time.

Listen to advice and store it. Some winter you may be glad your larder is full.

The second set of helpful counselors was a couple we barely knew. They invited us to their home for dinner. It wasn't a heavy or planned "session." As we joked that evening they dropped little hints of what had worked for them and what had not. No big deal, but it was such an uplifting look at marriage.

Many ministers now insist on premarital counseling. A few want one or two sessions of post-wedding counseling. Don't resist it. This is a gigantic improvement over the days when no one discussed it. Often the extent of sex counseling to the girl was merely "give yourself to your husband." Everyone figured the male didn't need any advice.

There are other professionals who can give excellent premarital counseling. However, ministers will be doing the bulk of it. If you have respect for your pastor, it can be a tremendous help.

Young couples are coming to appreciate this counseling. Frequently a couple will say, "We want marriage counseling." It has gained a good reputation and deserves it.

There are probably a score of other advisers available. Before we discuss them we should mention the best one: your partner. Each of us has a marriage counselor-in-residence. The smart couple counsels each other almost daily. "This is good." "This isn't working." "I really don't like tomatoes." "Red has always been my favorite color." "When we get a chance, I'd enjoy going out for dinner."

Dates for married couples make excellent therapy sessions. They are usually more convenient and often cheaper than going to professionals. The two of you go out for dinner and counsel each other. You tell her how beautiful her eyes look and say something nice about her clothes. That is good esteem-reinforcement. Make her feel good about herself.

She discusses her dream for adding an extra room on the house. This is dream-building and fosters hope for improvement. Tremendously healthy.

You tell her why a fishing vacation is the greatest. This is your chance to expand each other's horizons.

By going out for pie or a meal you have changed the setting. You have moved away from the immediate pressures and looked at them more objectively.

Many couples have changed the entire direction of their lives through date "therapy." By stepping outside their circumstances they were able to look it over and make a better decision.

There is one rule of date therapy which should be guarded tenaciously. Don't couple it with shopping. Many a husband can't stand shopping with his wife anyway. The very thought of it can wreck a date.

It sounds easy. The wife says, "Wonderful. While we are downtown we can stop in and look at some drapes." Count most husbands out. Just the thought of looking at material will give many men apoplexy.

Before you look high and low for good marriage counseling, ask yourself if you have checked at home. Don't assume you have. You may spend hours looking for an answer which your mate could have given you in five minutes.

There are two definite drawbacks to having your partner as counselor. There are some answers he honestly doesn't have. A couple doesn't always know enough to clear up every difficulty. When your lack of answers begins to damage your relationship, do not hesitate to seek other help.

The second difficulty is emotional involvement. Sometimes we are so close to the center of the problem we can't possibly be of help. Then we need another person who can look at the picture from a third perspective.

Not all good advice comes from people. Every engaged couple could be helped by familiarizing themselves with what the Bible says about marriage.

This is not suggested lightly. The Bible will give an up-front, honest view of what marriage is all about. It gives practical guidelines which can be applied to any marriage. Don't let the book's age deceive you. The Bible has an open, healthy concept of love.

Often the Bible has become buried under personal opinion. We listen to what people think the Bible says. The result is a misrepresented book. We end up with a cultural view rather than a factual one.

If you want to know what the Bible says about marriage, you must read it. I think you will find the Bible doesn't have the hangups some of us have.

Here are some passages you will want to read.

Sex—1 Cor. 7:1-7

In-laws—Eph. 5:31

Christian woman—Prov. 31

Love—1 Cor. 13

Submission—Eph. 5:21, 22

Another source of good advice is from a happily married couple. If you know a miserable couple, play "Password" with them, but don't look for clues. Their perspective is different. They have something to offer, but the total sum will probably be negative. Your view can become distorted in a hurry.

Happy couples are another story. They have problems and challenges. They also have fun.

Peg and Bob have a special relationship with her parents. Peg was brought up in a gregarious home where talking came easy. These newlyweds find it easy to talk with Peg's parents about marriage. Even intimate subjects are discussed with candor. If you can do this, by all means do. Parents have twenty to thirty years of good experience. It would be great to make use of some of this wisdom.

The same thing is true of other happily married couples. Just hanging around them is helpful. Their good qualities have a way of rubbing off almost like osmosis. Sometimes you want to ask these couples direct questions. Other times you benefit by watching them behave naturally.

Early in your experience it would be good to read a sex manual. There is nothing dirty about this if it is done correctly.

Despite the large publicity sex gets, there remains an enormous ignorance of the facts. Some individuals who are about to get married have only the vaguest concept of what intercourse is.

If all we know about sex is dirty jokes and handwriting on walls, we are in sad shape. A sex manual can be a marriage saver.

Get your first sex manual from your doctor. If he doesn't offer one, ask for it. They are informative and factual.

If you want to buy one from a store, do it later. Often these resemble gymnastics manuals more than love guides. They might be overwhelming for newlyweds.

Other books are valuable also. General guides to marriage can give excellent advice. New ones are coming out on the market continuously. They can be used to oil a few rusty spots.

Classes are also tremendous aids. If your church doesn't have a class on marriage, start lobbying now. You don't have to take it each time it is offered. However, it can help keep a marriage fresh.

Years ago these classes were unheard of. Marriage was supposed to be natural. Discussing it in groups was considered brash. Now we know marriage can use the help.

There are many couples who would like to raise the questions they have. They want to know how the others are handling things. Jump in on a class.

Marriage has suffered from too much romanticizing. At other times it grinds along from too little. Some partners did not really expect the ups and downs, smiles and tears which come with the package.

"I think I read too many books," said one girl. "They centered around the romance and selecting of homes and buying curtains. It all looked like a beautiful picture coming together stroke by stroke."

There may have been a few strokes she had not counted on.

Happiness is plentiful in marriage. Not only will it have the joys you counted on, but it holds many good surprises. The big problem is that happiness is not constant. But then none of the pleasures of life are constant. To accept this is the beginning of maturity.

Expect cross words, flare-ups, and even insults. They aren't the end of the world. Smart couples try to keep them to a minimum but they also know how to cushion them.

Place your hand on a table and try a little experiment. Palm down, press your left hand as tightly as possible. Now hit it hard with your right hand. If you hit it briskly it hurt.

Now let up with your left hand so it isn't pressed tightly on the table. Hit it. Your left hand hurts less because now it has give.

Marriage goes better with give. Sooner or later your partner will disappoint you. Learn to give with the bumps because the bumps are coming.

A woman with a list of complaints came to see me. She liked to go to bed at a certain time but her husband waited twenty more minutes to watch the news. He squeezed the toothpaste in the middle. It was all this type of thing.

Maybe she was extra tired that day. We discussed each "problem" and spent maybe fifteen minutes together. Nothing was earthshaking. She wasn't suffering from problems, she was suffering from life. Differences are as much a part of life as flowers, sunshine, and singing. She was a partner who needed to develop a little give. Not every cross wind is a tornado.

We listen to people describe their marriages like nursery rhymes. Everything is like clover.

What happened to your marriage? Your husband leaves his dirty socks on the chair. Your wife doesn't fix dessert half the time. Your lover goes to sleep on the couch and is zonked out when you want to go to bed. Then we bound off to a professional counselor to find out why our marriage doesn't measure up.

Don't become counselor-crazy. Not every tiff is worth a quick trip to a counselor. The smart partner knows the difference between normal and serious. Reading novels and seeing soap operas aren't good ways to find out.

It is hard to imagine now, but what if you do start to have deep problems? Something you feel you can't handle alone. No one knows if this will happen.

If a crack develops which only widens, don't hesitate to seek help. Many marriages could have been mended if the couple had not been too proud to admit their problems and ask for outside assistance.

Sometimes this is particularly true of Christians. We aren't supposed to have marital problems. Consequently, many try to cover them up instead of solving them. Many of those hidden difficulties are now coming to the top like erupting volcanoes.

Others develop problems and run to lawyers. They have accepted the amputation theory. If something is giving you a hard time, cut it off. It doesn't solve anything, but it will remove it.

Lawyers make lousy marriage counselors. If the average Christian has serious marital problems, the best person to seek for a solution is his pastor. Without becoming prejudiced, I really think this is an excellent start. Some ministers are terrible at marriage counseling. So are some counselors. However, the majority are good resource people.

Many ministers have extensive experience dealing with families. Often they are authorities on the root causes such as forgiveness, tolerance, flexibility, fear, and even communication.

But maybe your minister isn't a good counselor. He still could be the place to start. Ask him if he could refer you to someone. Most of us don't know a dependable counselor. We are reluctant to pick a name from the phone book. Ministers have names and experience working with marriage counselors.

On a number of occasions I have tried to recommend another minister. Some couples were reluctant because they felt they knew me too well. In some communities relatives are too thick and are part of the problem. It could be healthy to refer the partners to a pastor across town or in the next town.

No one has to feel hurt or sneaky. In some settings there will be greater freedom if you can get away.

A doctor and hospital administrator once paid the clergy a high compliment. I met him while serving my tour as a hospital chaplain.

"I have high regard for you ministers. A few years ago my wife and I were having a bad time. I don't go to church but my wife convinced me to try some counseling with a local minister. He never even mentioned the fact that I didn't go there. He really did a lot to save our marriage."

This open door attitude won't always be true. With the better pastors it will. If you want a marriage counselor or a psychologist, tell your minister. He wants what is best for you and will refer you.

Other Christians are very proud that they have never seen a marriage counselor. Some of these have been miserable for years. They will never find help. For them the name of the game is to keep looking good while they rot internally. Our compassion goes out to them.

Wherever you go to seek advice and counsel, there are a few guidelines to keep in mind. Even when there is a serious rift between you and your partner, certain rules abide. You have pledged your love to your mate. Now that things are rocky, don't turn and try to hurt him.

Some partners are angry and now trying to smear their mate. They have told the grocery clerk, bridge club, and dentist all about their difficulties. No matter how often you tell it, your partner comes out as the creature from the dark lagoon.

Cool it! This is nonproductive and cruel. This talk says more about the one speaking than the one being charged. Tell a professional or a confidant what the problem is. Be specific. Don't drag in every old gripe and imagined gripe over the past five years. Exaggerated charges only hinder a solution.

Aim for a solution! Some partners enjoy complaining about their spouse. It keeps their mind off the kids or the miserable job. Look for an answer.

My wife is sacred! There are times when I have not always appreciated her. A couple of times I wanted to wring her neck. But *never* have I wanted to make her look like a villain in front of my friends.

When I hear husbands speaking derogatorily about their wives, I cringe. My wife has loved me through storms and sunshine. She is the mother of my three children. She is too sacred to smear. I don't hold many things in life as untouchable, but my wife is one of them.

"Her children stand and bless her; so does her husband. He praises her with these words: 'There are many fine women in the world, but you are the best of them all'" (Prov. 31:28, 29).

If you are looking for good advice, don't just look for people who will agree with you. This doesn't solve anything; it only reinforces your position.

A few even go so far as to seek a counselor so they can feel free to divorce. Always determined to split, they can now say, "Well, I tried counseling but we didn't get anywhere."

It is hard to get "anywhere" when the person has his mind made up.

The best attitude toward advice is the search for help. A need to grow, learn, expand is at its heart. We are asking someone to help us see something we couldn't see before.

Many couples can't see the roots to their problems. We might think we have trouble communicating. In reality financial debts may leave us too depressed to talk. We might believe we are losing interest in sex. We may actually be too sick to care.

Talking it over can be a real eye opener. Find someone with patient ears, a little experience, and two tons of compassion.

"How does a man become wise? The first step is to trust and reverence the Lord! Only fools refuse to be taught. Listen to your father and mother. What you learn from them will stand you in good stead; it will gain you many honors" (Prov. 1:7-9).

11
HAUNTED HOUSES

"Before I met Jan my sex life was, well, active. Now that we are going to get married I wonder if I should tell her everything?"

Brad isn't the only person facing this dilemma. This is one of the questions most frequently asked by engaged couples. How much do you tell and when?

This is a complex problem. Don't assume that because you are Christians you should tell everything and the sooner the better. People are like snowflakes; no two are the same.

Isn't holding back the truth just the same as lying? They are definitely not the same. One night my back ached and I didn't tell my wife. I didn't lie about my back, but neither did I tell her everything.

The person who is just doggedly tastelessly determined to "let it all hang out" may be starting an avalanche he can't control.

Naturally, your partner needs to know anything that may affect your marriage. Have you been married previously? Do you have a child? Do you have a serious illness? Are there legal entanglements which may affect you? Do you have a prison record? Do you have a history of mental health problems?

These facts may not hurt your marriage at all. However, your partner has a right to know what to expect. In most cases the knowledge will only strengthen the relationship. If it can destroy the two of you, this is a good time to find out.

But don't try to shock. Don't exhume every sordid detail. It may be more than the person really wanted to know, at least for now.

This also means you would not lie to your partner. If he asks you a direct question it deserves a direct answer. But this doesn't mean you have to expound on the subject. If you ask me if I have ever walked up the Washington Monument you don't expect me to describe every step.

Does this mean you should never tell her or him about your past? By no means. It merely reminds us that not everything is worth blurting out.

Because you are a sensitive partner you learn to read the person you love. Is this a good time to discuss your activities while you were in the service? Maybe it is. Would a better time be two years from now when the two of you are sharing? A distinct possibility. Would the best time be never? Don't rule it out.

Back off and evaluate your situation. The "I have to tell everything" fever may not be helpful.

"I don't really care what his past was like. I know what he is like now." Sandra said it and she meant it. Later the conversation may turn naturally in that direction and she will want to know. Don't force her under the heat of "I have to tell all."

Barbara should know today. Henry would like to know six months from now. Sue can't quite handle it yet. Shawn doesn't care to ever know. Learn what your partner is like and respond lovingly.

Whether you and your partner have a checkered past or not, there are two anchors your marriage will need. They are twins called forgiving and forgetting.

The same high qualities which make you an excellent person will also make you a magnificent partner. If you find it easy to forgive, you are well down the halls toward happiness. Those who hold grudges and are set on getting even are heading for the pits.

If your mate is vengeful and unforgiving you are marrying a headache. Buy bottles of aspirin and a football helmet—you are going to need both.

The need for forgiveness will stretch like a wing across your married life. The couple who are long on it will climb like the eagles.

This forgiveness begins today. And it begins by forgiving yourselves. Many couples who have been engaged for very long have participated in some form of advanced sexual activity. It may be heavy petting or intercourse. It could also involve a number of other sexual activities.

If you have, are you going to let this haunt you? Many young couples do. After they have been married two, five, or fifteen years they are still carrying this ghost around. They have never accepted the forgiveness of God and under no circumstances do they plan to forgive each other.

Steve and Renee let their premarital sex activity practically rule their lives. She became pregnant and they got married. In their early years all they discussed was how they got into this mess. They often mentioned it to their friends. When their children began to grow, the parents started their war cry immediately. "Don't let the same thing happen to you that happened to us."

What a waste! They flunked the first test of happiness. They weren't able to forgive each other.

After you are married, sex will probably become less of a problem. Broken promises, exaggerations, and maybe even an occasional lie may become the patience stretchers.

Don't discount these little things. Many couples could not cope because they couldn't forgive and forget the small faults.

There was a funny movie in which a husband was looking at *Time* magazine and he, off the cuff, mentioned a picture of a pretty woman. The wife didn't think the remark was cute. In short order the incident mushroomed and they were both seeing their lawyer.

While you are handling the big problems, watch out. The little ones will creep up and shanghai you. Try to separate the incidences from the patterns. Once in a while your partner will be thoughtless. Don't blow this out of proportion.

Kathy has always been sensitive about the size of her nose. When I met her I didn't think it looked big, but she thinks so. Her husband Ron knew she worried too much, so he was careful not to mention it, even in kidding.

One day the couple was wrestling on the floor playfully and trading meaningless insults. Without thinking Ron said, "Let go of me, Hawk Nose."

Ron didn't come close to meaning it. He didn't even think it. It was careless, and in this case it was cruel.

This bothered Kathy, but fortunately, she was mature enough to let it ride. Her first reaction was, "You dog!" but she held back. Later she said how glad she was she let the remark bounce off rather than going to war over it.

Throw the small pebbles off immediately. They get flung all the time and are not worth the bother. If you keep each pebble, they soon start to weigh a ton. Forgive and forget immediately.

When it comes to patterns, it may be a different story.

There was a newlywed who had a habit. She kept leaving the bottom dresser drawer open. No big deal. Every morning she gave it a half push and it stuck out about six inches.

Her husband worked hard at being Prince Charming. Each morning he cracked his shin on the drawer. It smarted terribly but he wouldn't say anything. While one hand held his shin the other one would politely close the drawer. He said nothing and she left it open for two months.

One morning he cracked his shin for the fortieth time and wheeled in one motion and belted his wife. He saw a pattern in his wife but he refused to deal directly and kindly with the situation. They could have discussed the problem, adjusted their behavior, hugged, and forgotten it. But because of his refusal to deal with an obvious pattern it became explosive.

Some behavior cannot be forgiven or forgotten until it is faced. If he leaves his socks where you do not like it once or twice, let it ride. When he does it all the time, talk. If a certain behavior still bugs you, it is not forgiven or forgotten. Fools put blankets over fires without making sure they are out. Smart partners love each other enough to deal with dangerous patterns.

Your home is going to be an open, forgiving environment. Most people who care enough to prepare for marriage are careful enough to work on forgiveness.

Working on forgiveness is the right way to put it. Forgiveness doesn't fall automatically from heaven. If this were the case, the Bible would not have to tell us to do it. Forgiveness is not a trait we are born practicing. Some people can forgive more easily than others because they have practiced it more often.

The Bible merely tells us to stop being harsh and start being kind: "Stop being mean, bad-tempered and angry. Quarreling, harsh words, and dislike of others should have no place in your lives. Instead, be kind to each other, tenderhearted, forgiving one another, just as God has forgiven you because you belong to Christ" (Eph. 4:31, 32).

Again, the same qualities which make a good person are the ones which make a good marriage.

It is up to you to set the pace. Accept that responsibility. We have an enormous effect on our partner. Don't wait for your mate to establish the rules for forgiveness. If you set a high standard of forgiveness, most partners will respond in kind. That is great news for you.

Practice needs to begin now. How are you handling the demands of engagement? What do you do when he is late? How do you feel when he picks the wrong restaurant? What is your reaction when he says something which is thoughtless or crude?

Don't be tied to your past performance. Maybe you have not found forgiveness easy as you were growing up. Possibly it was not popular in your family. Too many young people shrug their shoulders and say, "Well, I am what I am." Here is good news—that isn't true. Forgiveness is a skill perfected by practice. Because you care you will be more forgiving next year than you are this year.

Because you are more forgiving you can watch your partner blossom like a giant sunflower.

Couples can misuse forgiveness, and a few of these problems should be mentioned: Don't become confession-happy. Some partners have a driving urge to tell everything and ask forgiveness. Continuous self-inspection is a miserable, neurotic route to travel. Ed said he sold a dozen but really only sold eleven. Now he has to straighten it out. He glared at a woman in the drugstore and now feels guilty.

Don't make confession an excuse for sinning. You could scrape open more wounds than you heal. The human mind is capable of devious plots. Some are so clever we are not even aware of them.

Since forgiveness comes readily, we may grow to depend on it. What does it matter if I do this? My mate will forgive me.

All of us do this sometimes, but be careful. At its heart it is cruel. "I won't call to tell her I'll be late. She will probably get mad, but she will forgive me."

We need to guard ourselves from taking advantage of kindness. Too much presumption and we may dull the edge.

Another important don't—don't use forgiveness as a hostage. Many of us are still childish enough to play this game. Our mate has obviously done something stupid. He would like to make it right and get it off his conscience. We see it as a way to gain something. Instead of generously forgiving, we withdraw and act cold. This is holding forgiveness hostage. In marriage it is definitely criminal.

I am sure you would never do that. But don't be too sure what a sinful mind will do—even one which is in love.

You will be tempted to think about how you wanted the kitchen painted. When will you ever get a new dress? He might want to go hunting next week. If you withhold your forgiveness, stay cool—maybe you will get some goodies out of this deal.

There is a basic rule about generosity. When we are kind we end up the ultimate beneficiaries.

"It is possible to give away and become richer! It is also possible to hold on too tightly and lose everything. Yes, the liberal man shall be rich! By watering others, he waters himself" (Prov. 11:24, 25).

This rule also applies to forgiveness.

The key word to forgiveness is mercy. If you keep records or are waiting to get even, forgiveness becomes a meaningless mush. We all forgive; after all, we are Christians. It is also possible for this word to become a hollow barrel. If we do not forgive in fact, we do not forgive at all. Just hurling out words proves nothing.

Mercy, not justice, is the key. Be a burden lifter. Your mate will sometimes have stooped shoulders from what he has done or said. That is when it is so great to have a terrific mate like you. Your love will lift the tons straight off his back. Do it quickly. Do it often. Do it without reservation.

After we have forgiven our partner the really hard work begins. How in the world can you forget? Especially if it has cut deeply and you have bled profusely?

You can't keep dredging it up either verbally or mentally. It deserves a decent burial.

Forgetting comes in degrees. There are some things which I no longer remember and yet I have not forgotten them. (I hope that sentence will make sense to you later.)

I remember the Second World War (just barely, please). I know how the Asian campaign ended. I recall when President Truman announced it to the world. All sorts of facts and images float around in the back of my brain.

However, I do not remember the war like white heat. I don't hate the Japanese or the Germans. I don't look for their labels on products and refuse to buy them.

Forget the war? Impossible. Forget the intense hate and damage? Now there is an order I can fill.

Your marriage will never become World War II, but some of the principles are the same. If a husband has an affair with another woman, I doubt that the wife totally forgets it. Yet, she can bring herself to the place where it no longer vibrates. It is no longer an emotional issue. She remembers it only as an unfortunate part of history.

If you store memories you may be merely postponing the explosion. Some memories are good for laughs. Even though they hurt at the time, they are funny today. Not every memory can be funny, but all memories—all memories—can be diffused. They are diffused by genuine forgiveness.

When two partners flood their marriage with forgiveness they can hardly miss.

Have a fantastic marriage.

12
MIXED COUPLES

Every partner should know what he is getting into. Marriage has enough surprises without ignoring the facts.

What are the odds of success for your type of union? Once you learn what you are up against, you may choose to go full steam ahead. You are not the national average. You are one couple and must weigh your own circumstances.

A general rule says the more a couple has in common the better the chance of success. They can have many differences and still be happy. However, their glue comes from like interests.

There are three major areas of differences: religion, race, and nationality. The biggest problem of these three remains mixed religions.

If two dedicated believers from separate religions marry they are likely to have trouble. If a dedicated believer marries a religiously cold or hostile partner, there will probably be difficulty no matter what the religion.

Write those two maxims on the back of your hand. Read them all day long. Most people who ignore them live to regret it.

It becomes a different story if one of the partners changes. Many of these switches work out beautifully.

Before you get married, resolve the serious questions of your faith. Don't tell yourself you will iron them out later. Often later makes it more difficult.

There is more to settle than just the obvious questions. Both of you need to know where you stand in your faith in Jesus Christ. Listen to each other. Don't just look for a key word or magic phrase. Discuss the subject and hear what your partner means. Some beautiful Christians have rejected great partners because they never heard the right sentence. Others have married duds because they used a familiar terminology.

It may be difficult to talk about your Christian faith to someone you love very much. (Often it is easier with a stranger.) Work at it. It is something you need to discuss the rest of your life. You can walk around some streams, but this one you have to cross.

This is both a sociological problem and a Christian problem. Most people still marry within their own religious framework.

Suppose a Protestant and a Catholic marry. If one does not change over, a point of separation has to occur. From a practical side, where do you go to church? Maybe you will go one Sunday to hers and the next Sunday to his. Can you be content attending your church only half the time?

A couple will decide to attend his church at 9:00 and hers at 11:00. It is a possibility. How will you raise your children? Will they attend both? Will they eventually attend neither?

This sounds like a mechanical problem. However, other questions could become more intense later. How will your child be baptized? Is infant baptism important to you? Will it insult your partner? What does communion mean to you?

You can handle those "little things" later. That is what many couples think. Later they find them completely impassable. Cold water is poured on their marriage.

Bring your differences down to closer quarters. Methodists and Baptists. Presbyterian and Assembly of God. How do you feel about baptism, charismatics, eternal life, Sunday school, and even Bible translations?

There are married couples who do not discuss their Christian faith because they find their differences insurmountable. The more you solve now the greater your compatibility later.

Suppose your problem is even more serious. Can a Christian marry a non-Christian and be happy? Without talking to every couple, you have to think it is highly doubtful.

As a Christian, you acknowledge that Jesus Christ is essential to your life. Can you be content not to discuss something this vital with your spouse? Can you rope it off as untouchable?

The Bible is unyielding in its warning against the unequal yoke. In the Old Testament the theme echoed. Don't marry a nonbeliever. The New Testament stands just as firmly.

"Don't be teamed with those who do not love the Lord, for what do the people of God have in common with the people of sin?" (2 Cor. 6:14).

A smart partner will also ask a second question. Are my mate and I on the same level of Christian commitment? Just being a Christian may not be enough.

I meet Christian couples who are miserable. He wants to head the youth group and start a home Bible study. She wants to go on Sunday mornings and forget it. There is a continuous friction between them.

She wants to feed the hungry. He has never parted with a dime. If you want to express your Christian faith, don't marry Mount Rushmore. Everytime you want to serve, your partner sits like a rock.

The levels of commitment don't have to be identical. You will be far better off if they are similar.

When you are trying to develop your marriage along Christian guidelines, don't be a carbon copy. We hear of couples who pray and read the Bible together daily. This may be great for you and it may not. Many couples pray well and seldom pray together. Work out your Christian life as it best suits the two of you. Some couples are miserable because they are trying to match someone else's model. There is great width in Christian expression, and you should feel free to exercise it.

After you are satisfied with your Christian compatibility, double check your concept of roles in marriage. As we discuss in the chapter on Future Family, the roles of husband and wife are changing. Half the married women are now working outside the home. Be sure both of you have a close agreement of the roles you will play.

If you have seriously mixed views, painful friction can result.

In his mind he may be thinking you are going to work. All the time you have been dreaming of quiet afternoons spent making curtains. It is far saner to resolve these dreams now than to try later.

Lifetime situations do not have to be engraved in concrete. Both of you may change your minds later. However, any strong feelings could use airing now. Don't later find yourself in a box when you didn't realize it.

The number of interracial marriages in the United States is on the increase. It still is not a major factor in the total population, but it could become one.

This situation isn't a "problem" in all parts of the world. In some countries interracial marriage is an accepted practice.

Twenty years ago it was illegal in forty states in this country. In one state a couple could be sentenced to two years in prison for mixing the races. Often the minister or judge was fined for conducting the service.

As recently as 1967 the Supreme Court ruled these laws to be unconstitutional. It is important for all of us to know how strong these feelings have been.

Not long ago a biracial couple went hunting for an apartment in a large city. All the advertised rentals had just been filled. Afterward one of the partners went looking and soon had a place.

The laws have changed, but in many places the feelings have not.

Figures have jumped during the past ten to fifteen years. They have actually grown more than we know since many states no longer require race designation on a marriage license.

There are at least 250,000 biracial marriages in the United States. In cases in which a black and white marry, the male is the black partner four times more frequently than the female.

Several surveys indicate biracial marriages are no more or less stable than the general population. Their divorce rate is approximately the same. Interracial partners may have an added resolve to make it go. They also may work harder to fortify each other.

These statistics do not tell a biracial couple whether or not to marry. They are merely aimed at letting you know where the situation presently stands. We should also remember that we are only a few years advanced from official condemnation of the practice.

If you are considering a biracial marriage there are at least three problems to weigh: the Bible problem, the social problem, and the children problem.

The Bible problem is no problem. There are a few who think they can prove God never wanted biracial marriage. The biblical problem simply doesn't exist.

God is concerned about Christians marrying nonbelievers. People seem more concerned about biracial marriages. If God did not want interracial couples he was capable of flatly saying so. The Bible problem is no problem.

The social problem is as tough as nails. We live in a society which is not ready to accept this. It is more tolerant than twenty years ago, but far from accepting. Some surveys suggest it is better accepted in black communities, but there is no enthusiasm.

Sin seems to have convinced us we are better than others. As long as any race believes this, there will be difficulty.

Don't think the problem is merely black and white. In many areas, marrying a Mexican, Japanese, or Filipino is greeted with equal hostility. Some communities, however, accept it warmly.

Many families (Christian and non-) will find the situation intolerable. The marriage will be more painful than most can handle.

It is a problem we should all be ashamed of. Our deep-rooted prejudices are testimonies to our true nature.

Are you going with a person of a different race? No one can tell you to marry or not. As Christians we should be committed to support your decision.

Don't be naive as to what you face. Most will meet housing discrimination. Many will get strange if not dirty looks the rest of their lives. There may be considerable subtle job discrimination. Your partner will occasionally be treated as socially unacceptable.

There are couples who are facing these problems squarely. They are married, happy, and well adjusted. It can be done and is done. The smart biracial partners have met their difficulties head on.

The children problem cannot be ignored. You are not making this decision for yourself alone. If you choose to have children, they will have their own set of challenges. Can you prepare them? Will you take time to mold them?

These are all heavy decisions to make. If at all possible it would help to discuss them with a biracial couple. Their experiences, good and bad, should shed light on the sharp turns ahead.

An understanding group of Christians would be a big help. Their support and acceptance could lighten your load considerably.

We do know Moses evidently married an Ethiopian woman. When Aaron and Miriam objected to the union, God inflicted Miriam with leprosy (Num. 12:1).

Many of us still suffer from a racial superiority complex. It has not passed quickly or well.

There are several specific traps to avoid. Don't go into an interracial or any other marriage just to prove anything. A young lady thinks, "I'll show my mother I can make decisions without her. When I marry this man she will see." If you can sense this in yourself, put on the brakes now.

Never marry anyone as a social statement. Don't be the martyr who is going to bring a halt to social injustice. Support a political candidate, work in the ghetto, become a social worker. Marriage makes a lousy platform.

Occasionally a couple is mixed drastically by age. Possibly eight to twenty years separate the partners. These marriages do not occur frequently enough to establish a dependable pattern.

It is fair to say that many of these marriages are tremendously happy. They allow for the advantages and disadvantages of their separate ages.

Simple arithmetic will answer many of their questions. Suppose they marry at twenty and forty. Will they still be compatible at thirty and fifty? What about forty and sixty?

How will this affect your attitude toward children? The likelihood you will be a widow or widower is greatly increased.

Not all of these difficulties can be solved with a simple "we love each other." Special qualities are necessary to make this a beautiful match.

Marriage is too personal to merely draw lines. To say this type of marriage will be happy and this one sad is a gross oversimplification.

There is a strong possibility Joseph was quite a few years older than Mary. We can't say for certain. We do know God considered the marriage a good risk.

A couple I knew truly loved each other. Their eyes sparkled and they enjoyed just being in the same universe. She told me, "I'm so relieved Warren is three weeks older than me. If he had been three weeks younger than me I probably wouldn't have married him."

The age question has become overly important to some otherwise clear-thinking people. Twenty years difference may be vital. Two or three can't mean much.

While we are discussing the age factor, we can also look at teenage marriages. Here we do know the risks are great.

There is a myth going around that people a few generations ago married as teenagers. Actually our grandparents may have married slightly younger than we do, but only slightly. Most couples a hundred years ago married in their early twenties.

Teenage marriage has always been difficult in our society. It is rough to determine which factors make it hard. We can say with authority that the average teenage marriage faces a treacherous route.

The present divorce rate is six times higher among those who married under twenty-one. In these breakups, age does not seem to be the only problem. However, it is a scary prospect for the young to face.

There are often some definite advantages. Partners can mold ideas together. They can begin to plan their future with an early start. Raising children is usually easier when parents are younger.

These are advantages for couples in their early twenties. Often they become disadvantages under twenty.

Possibly our society should not be this way. But it is. The broken marriages prove the dangers involved.

If you are a teenager you will be hard to convince. This is easy to understand, especially if you have picked out a potential partner.

You probably know couples who were married at sixteen, and twenty years later they are happy as chipmunks. But don't bet your marriage on it. A huge number do not work out.

If you can wait, do. The "I have to get married now" feeling is better off harnessed. Let your life develop a bit more and you may be able to handle a healthy marriage even better.

Don't let the sexual pressure push you into marriage. Get some hobbies and other interests. Sex is not enough reason to get married.

Pregnancy is *never* enough reason to marry. If all you have in common is the ability to reproduce, you are both in deep trouble.

13

DO YOU WANT CHILDREN?

Is this too early to discuss children? You probably aren't even married yet. There are more pressing questions like which cakes, flowers, and shoe colors to choose. In the middle of all these decisions, take a few minutes and check out some attitudes. They will be tremendously valuable during the next two years—and maybe longer.

Doesn't everyone want children? Not now. There was a time when young couples automatically planned on half a dozen offspring. Today there are decisions to make and alternatives to weigh. You not only have the question of how many, but whether you are to have any at all.

There is one decision which has to be made now. If your mate is vehemently against having children, do you want to marry him? If your potential partner is cool or indifferent you may have someone to work with. However, if he is immovable, now is the time to ask if you are prepared to marry someone who "hates" children. This is too big a difference to ignore.

Since this seldom happens, we won't linger on the possibility. But, if it is the case, resolve this issue before the final ring is slipped in place.

Other degrees of differences aren't worth worrying about. When I first got married, children weren't exactly a high priority. I wanted to marry the girl I loved, but little crying creatures weren't what I had in mind. After two years of marriage we had gotten to know each other and were ready for a pink bundle.

This growth is natural when two people are pliable. They are open to make decisions together. Now we have three large bundles.

Most likely you will have children. Whether by plan or by accident, this is still the way it works out. Generally couples have fewer children (around two or three) than their grandparents or even parents. The numbers have reduced as we have become more concerned about zero population growth. Inflation, housing, and double careers are also making a difference.

This isn't all bad. Not everyone has to have children and certainly we don't have to have six in each family. The birth of children should be a joy and not an obligation.

We are free to have children. We are also free not to have them.

The Bible tells us to multiply and fill up the earth. Give us credit. We have done a great job of this. We may have flunked the Great Commission, feeding the hungry, and making peace—but multiply—we have done a fantastic job. We can feel relaxed and accomplished.

If my wife and I had our lives to live over, we would have children again. (This will come as good news to our trio.) These are our reasons. They might help you too.

Children have definitely made our triangle of love complete. (Don't ask how a family of five becomes a triangle.) My wife and I greatly enjoyed our first two years together. Being newlyweds can be both trying and a blast. After a while we started to feel a need for our love to reach out. It needed a third dimension.

This won't happen to everyone. I know couples who have no children and find their third dimension in other ways. They spend their mutual love on young people and Christian work. There is no doubt they are happy, dedicated, and perfectly comfortable.

For most couples this doesn't work. They become saturated with themselves and need an outlet. A natural avenue is to have a child. It is a God-given outlet.

Having a child is a self-fulfilling adventure. You feel you have something to give. You also want something in return. Just the fact that it is satisfying doesn't make it work. A child meets your needs and at the same time becomes a vehicle to express love. It doesn't sound all bad.

Another reason we decided on children was Pat's need to create. This is easier for women to understand than men. It is one thing to hold someone else's child. This alone seems to light up the eyes of most women. However, it is entirely different to be able to snuggle your own. A woman realizes that her body has created a human being. The baby may have her eyes or her husband's chin. Either way it is a product of her body, care, and love.

Anyone who has created artistically approaches the same sensation. The canvas, woodwork, metal sculpture are the result of a combined effort as a person brings all of his abilities to bear. Motherhood is similar.

If it is inconvenient, and even painful, most mothers think it is worth it. Many decide to give birth two, three, or four times.

Often it means even more when the woman has chosen motherhood in her own time. She controls her births and spaces her creative act as she can best handle it. But those surprise creations can be real heartwarmers too.

We also wanted our own little litter because they are tremendously interesting. A fish bowl can't even compare. Wind-up toys are dull by this standard. Children make a fascinating hobby.

Both of us had tried roller-coasters, pistol practice, touch football, and theater going. None of those activities is a match for the amazing life of raising children.

Every day they change and grow. They become more complicated. But with each turn they show an interesting side we had not seen before.

Sometimes it is painful to raise children. They become a responsibility which you can't enjoy every day. Most good things are that way. An automobile is a big help and a continuous responsibility. So is a house, a job, and a trip to Denver.

Children are far more pleasure than they are pain. There are exceptions to this, but not for most of us. Sometimes we exaggerate the ill effects. Usually they are like a steady rain. They leave far more than they take.

When a couple starts to complain too much about the strain, they have begun to distort the picture. Raising children has supposedly cost them this and cost them that. Don't ever lose sight of what our children have given to us. Our lives are rich because our children have given us their wealth.

When the children were infants we didn't want them to grow up. They were so dependent, innocent, and cute. If they had become toilet trained and swore off crying, we would have kept them just that way.

Then they started to grow and new worlds opened up to us. Talking was a fascinating experience. Walking was similar to a funny tornado. Then the first day of school. We bought Mary a bookbag so large she could barely carry it. Our kindergartner was going to be prepared. (Previously we had bought her a microscope which even her parents couldn't operate.)

Each age was more amazing than the previous. On three or four nights we cried. On thousands we smiled, laughed, or giggled.

A pretty television hostess told 30 million people she would be afraid to raise children in this society. She probably was speaking for many young people. For all its benefits this is a dangerous world. Drugs, alcohol, war, cancer, divorce, murder, rape, robbery, inflation are each taking a terrible toll. No one dares deny this, especially if tragedy has hit close to your family.

However, it is a bit early to throw in the towel. Our grandparents had plenty of reasons not to raise children, too. Many families lived miles from the nearest doctor. World War I was hovering like a vampire bat. Plagues of grasshoppers had stripped the land.

Then came the depression. World War II erased many young men—husbands and fathers.

It can be a tough world. This has always been a dangerous place to live. We can't sit in our homes, lock the doors, and say there might be a lion in the street (Prov. 26:13). To do this is to give up life.

There is risk in raising children. Most of us think we can't afford them. More than likely our parents, grandparents, and great-grandparents couldn't afford it either. Children are an enormous financial investment. All they have to offer in return is love, warmth, and hope.

Children are an excellent expression of hope. We believe in tomorrow and God's ability to work in this world. If he can use our children to carry out his plan, all the better.

Within reason, your children may help dispel some of the gigantic problems we face. Your child may discover solutions to the need for food. He might find a cure for cancer.

Maybe your child will work in a gas station and never get his name in the paper. But by the grace of God that will be a better gas station because your child is there.

Christ has invited us to be the salt of the earth. Our children can help a world rather than become its burden. With this attitude a couple has no reason to fear having a manageable number of children.

This is just a start. You can add your own list of good reasons to have children. They are important to spell out so you don't lose your bearings.

All of these same benefits can come by adopting. Even the desire to be a creative mother can be satisfied by adoption. Your body will not give birth but you will still shape a life with your love, concern, and healthy standards.

Because of the present laws about abortion, adoption is often difficult. However, it is done, and often. Many are giving good homes to foreign and mixed-racial children.

Adopting does not prohibit you from giving birth. A few couples have adopted the first, and given birth to the second by choice. Others adopt the first and are surprised by a pregnancy. Either way it can be exciting.

If there are good reasons to have children, there are a few bummers around too. Check these off quickly and avoid them.

Never have children to satisfy anyone else. This sounds silly but it is real. Some couples become tired of being asked, "Haven't you started your family yet?" Talkative neighbors and well meaning friends are prone to say dumb and empty things. Don't let this pressure you into having a child before you are ready.

Never have children to create a work force. A hundred years ago this was frequently discussed. Don't raise children to milk cows or tend a store.

Never have children to satisfy your parents. They might enjoy becoming grandparents, but it must be your decision. Grandparents visit the child; you have to live with him. It is a subtle pressure which can become tons of weight. Have a child only when *you* are ready.

Never try to make up for your lost childhood. Maybe you were underprivileged or disadvantaged. Possibly you felt you lacked love and attention as you grew up. Now you want to pour love on your own child.

Under these conditions he can become a real brat. This type of handicap he doesn't need.

Never have a child to prove yourself a woman or a man. A few people are terribly confused about maturity. They believe an event will qualify them as an adult.

Having a child can prove nothing except that your body is working properly. Responsible action says something about our maturity. Having children only proves you can reproduce.

Never have a child to save a marriage. Instead of solving your problems it could multiply them. You probably know a case in which a child has saved a marriage. But there are also many times when it grew from a marriage problem into a family disaster.

The child has been used as a medicine. If the cure fails to take, the child ends up getting hurt. It is too much of a gamble to take.

Find other help for your marital rift. Then bring a bouncing baby into a happy home. The rewards are far greater this way.

Never have a child because you did not adequately understand or use birth control. Birth by accident can be enjoyable. Birth by plan is fantastic.

If you decide to have children (and almost all of you will), there are some attitudes to work out now. The attitudes are more important than the actions. Attitudes will ultimately control what we do.

Promise yourself that you will keep your life balanced. Parents are prone to two extremes. One group is self-centered, leaving the children to raise themselves. Another group is child-centered and everything revolves around making the child's life ideal.

Both extremes are disastrous. If you have to choose between one or the other, don't. They are both the pits.

The first problem is abandonment-in-residence. Their children have been left to grow up by themselves.

Have you met couples who were into every activity in the world except raising children? They cannot say no, basically because they don't want to say no. If they need a chairman for the Save The Pebble committee, you can count on them.

It is almost as if we are embarrassed to say, "I need time to raise my children." This has to be a high priority among parents.

A woman told me about all the people who are influencing her son. The fact is no one—no one—has as much influence over your children as you do. Not if you want that influence.

Parents have four hours a night plus twelve hours on Saturday and twelve on Sunday. That is forty-four hours. No teacher, television set, or friend spends that much time with our child.

If everything else has priority in our lives, our children will be left to be raised by others. Don't be content with that.

The other problem is to center our life on our children. Everything revolves around them.

The happiness of our child becomes not only our major concern but often our only one. This is no exaggeration.

111

Linda was this type of mother and she was fed up with her family. On Mondays she took them to piano, Tuesdays was 4-H, Wednesdays was Awana, Thursdays was basketball, Friday was a slumber party. If it rained she drove two paper route deliverers.

She had no life of her own. Their wish had become her command. Life was dull and meaningless. She was living for her children and them alone.

Such parents often divorce at forty. When their children leave, their world collapses. Over the years the partners have lost all their mutual interests. Now they are alone with nothing in common. They decide to start life all over again.

Children suffer from too much neglect. Children also suffer from too much attention. Unhappy parents usually contribute to making unhappy children.

Determine you will raise your child for himself and not for everyone else. This is one of the most difficult tasks in parenthood.

One day we were faced squarely with this problem. Our oldest girl asked if she could go to see a children's movie. If she had known what a crisis this presented she surely would not have asked. Many of our close Christian friends thought this was one of the worst things a person could do. To complicate matters, they were highly vocal.

Finally we came to this conclusion: for us to raise our children to please others was immoral.

The important question was whether the movie was good or bad for our girl. Neither the community nor our friends nor our church could raise our children. God put the responsibility squarely on us and we had to accept it.

Some of the problems we have reaped from children have come because we have spent too much time studying them. One writer says we have trouble because we do not spank our children. The next says we raise monsters because we do spank. A third authority blames it all on toilet training techniques.

There are some excellent books about training children. Read a couple and give it up. Confusion prevents many parents from directing their children. Decide on a path and follow it with determination.

Many parents are intimidated by their children. We are afraid they will not love us if we draw lines for them. Our goal should be gaining respect. Love will be much easier to collect once we have their attention.

The number of children you have will depend on choice, career, and health. In junior high school twelve might seem like fun. High school students might dream of six. Most married couples are now thinking in terms of two or three.

Start off with your picture of an ideal family. Maybe it is two or possibly ten. Keep your options open and go one at a time (if you can).

One couple had planned on a neat family of three children. Their third child was triplets and they found themselves an instant family of seven.

If you decide to pursue a career (and most women will) your package of children will probably be a small one. However, this does not have to be true. There is a woman at the local university who has a doctor's degree and five children. Don't try to match anyone. Your preferences and health are the important factors.

Generally women will want to complete their family by their early or mid-thirties. Talk this over with your doctor. The older you become the more complications are possible for both you and the child. All of us know someone who gave birth at forty or older. That doesn't change the facts. It is wise to consult your doctor before taking this risk.

Frequently, couples will say how thinly worn their nerves are after thirty. It is healthy for everyone involved to aim at parenthood earlier.

Having children early presents its challenges too. Usually a couple is trying to become settled. They are saving for the down payment on a house. Maybe they are finishing school or starting a career.

Within these boundaries their time is limited. Consequently, the family is often just as confined.

There is nothing wrong with this. Life styles change and so do the size of families.

Along with the number of children, you must ask how far apart you want them. Probably the biggest reason we did not have four is because we had three preschoolers at once. We seemed to be taking great risks with my wife's sanity. Since we were also thirty at the time, we decided to restrict the population. (Add to this the fact that one grandmother threatened my life.)

It is nice to have children a couple of years or more apart. This has to be good for the wife's body. It also gives everyone a chance to adjust to the new arrival and for the baby to become acquainted with us.

This is one of the few things we did right. We had a child every two years, each time in October ('64, '66, '68). My wife has never felt adequately honored for this feat.

14

YOU CAN NEVER
GO HOME

Your marriage is off to a fantastic start. Even before you say your
vows, the two of you are building together. You are making careful
plans, adjusting your attitudes, and learning about this new relationship.

Marriage will be for you a final step. Some couples eventually separate. Most likely this will not happen to you. Despite all the publicity given divorce, 80 percent of the population is still involved in
one partner marriages. The odds are great that your union is one of
these. The odds are even better if you both are Christians consciously
constructing your marriage.

After you say "I do," you will launch into a different relationship.
There will be no turning back. There will be no escape to the left
or the right. You will become two people in a lifeboat. There is no
place else to go, so you will sail together.

That is a great feeling. Your job is well defined. Since you can't
get out, you work at making the trip an ocean voyage. Kick off your
shoes, open a can of rations, sing together. This is going to be a good
cruise—all the way.

Before you cast off, there are a few questions you will want to ask
yourselves. If at all possible, both of you answer these. Some of them
might seem silly, but each has a purpose.

If you have to answer some of them "no," don't despair. It would help to talk these over and grow. If you answer a large number in the negative, you have a situation to stop and think about.

ARE YOU READY FOR A COMMITMENT?

An adult would have to think twice before he entered a room with no exits. Essentially this is what you are doing.

Don't be concerned if you have some doubts about this. Most of us probably do. Some days you may not be sure which way you are going to run.

However, if you really don't want to be tied down, now is the time to say so. Once in a while we meet the person who is running and almost never goes home. He wants to do whatever he wants to do. This person loves liberty but has no understanding of commitment.

You cannot be married and single. In order to be two, you must stop being one. Are you ready for this?

'Till death do us part could be a long time. Orville and Anna McVay have been married for almost sixty years. They love each other like kids. You might be married this long, too. Only those who fully expect to be have any business getting married.

Marriage is not a trial. It isn't a foreign dish to be sampled to see if it is tasty.

Will your commitment hold through sickness and health? Health is no problem. When you can hike, jog, play tennis, and go skiing, there is no strain. When you can love like Greek athletes, why should you worry?

What will happen if that body begins to quit? Not a pleasant thought, but it is part of the package.

Years ago I met a man bedridden with tuberculosis. He had been there for some time. When the diagnosis was certain, his wife sued for divorce. She couldn't be shackled to this.

I also read an article about a military officer whose wife contracted leprosy. She was admitted to a hospital in Louisiana. The officer resigned his commission and moved to be near her.

Which partner are you prepared to be? Love can be fickle. Commitment does not move.

Plenty and want are also uneven roads. The way of plenty must be the easier, but it isn't always. Many couples split over prosperity. Success can be just as difficult to handle as failure. The multimillionaire Mrs. Horace Dodge said her happiest days were when she was packing Horace's lunch bucket.

Suppose you do become president of the corporation. Maybe you will be professor of whatever. Will the pressures of a full life cause you to neglect each other? Many couples have said no and later forgot.

Pity the pains of poverty. There is a myth going around which claims that hardship draws people closer together. Don't count on it. Continuous debt and financial uncertainty take their toll.

What happens when you lose a good job and can no longer make the payments? It probably will never happen. But what if it does? Are you making a commitment which will last through changing conditions and pressures?

"Many waters cannot quench the flame of love, neither can the floods drown it. If a man tried to buy it with everything he owned, he couldn't do it" (Song 8:7).

ARE YOU WILLING TO WORK AT MARRIAGE?

What does work mean? To work is simply to spend energy. For marriage to rise to its beautiful potential, both of you will have to pour out energy.

Don't make it sound like a chain gang. Much of marriage really falls together. When love is a motivating factor it is amazing how well two people fit.

After a few months some couples are surprised that this will take more work than they expected.

A young man who had been married about six months said, "Sometimes I wonder why I bothered. The rest of the time it's fun."

Another married man put it this way, "I'll tell you what the difference is between dating and being married. With the first you are totally frustrated. In the second you are only partially frustrated."

Marriage is not grin and bear it. Neither is it all grin.

Suppose one of your early decisions is about having children. One wants to have a child after one year. The other wants to wait two. This one sounds easy. Love will certainly win out. Or so it appears.

Don't be surprised if it takes the State Department to negotiate this one. It may take long hours of discussions, agreements, bargaining, and promises before a treaty can be signed.

The entire process may be loving, but it also can be taxing. Couples do not automatically agree. Their willingness to work at it makes all the difference.

Be frank with yourself. Are you used to giving and taking? Have you had things pretty much your way so far?

Working together in an intimate relationship will take a diplomatic and learning attitude. The more you use these skills the stronger your marriage structure will become.

WILL THIS BE YOUR HOME?

Early in our marriage I asked my wife if she ever thought of leaving and going home. She said, "I am home."

For some this transition in thinking won't be difficult at all. Others will find it tempting to look back at their parents' home as paradise lost.

There was a man who dreaded becoming twenty-one. He knew he could no longer blame his mistakes on his being young. Some hate to get married for the same reason: they can no longer lean on their parents. A new relationship has begun and they must stand on their own.

Even married couples occasionally ask their parents for advice. If they are smart, they don't do it often. If the parents have good sense, they give it less.

Couples who are not ready to leave their former home and start their new one are not ready to marry. When you say your vows, turn in your old keys.

Suppose you can accept this fact but your parents can't. A few parents offer too much advice. They are continuously defending their poor child. If this happens to you, don't let it.

One young man politely but firmly drew the line with his own parents. They continuously dropped household, economic, and recreational "hints." Finally he confronted them. "You have to quit this. You are driving Angie nuts." They didn't like it, but they backed off.

The husband proved he was weaned. Now he had to kindly convince his parents.

Are you ready to burn a cake? Are you ready to hang wallpaper crooked? Are you ready to buy a cheap piece of furniture? Are you ready to make your own mistakes and build your own life? Then you may be ready to get married.

Welcome home!

IS THIS PURELY A PHYSICAL MARRIAGE?

Are you marrying a body or a person? It is fantastic to marry a person who also happens to be a body. It is tragic to marry a body who happens to be a person.

Don't take this question lightly. There are some young people who are so aroused physically they are ready to marry anyone.

If you marry someone merely because you need a warm body next to you, you may wish you had bought a cat or dog instead. Sooner or later you are going to have to get up and eat breakfast. What will you have in common then? What will you talk about? What kind of life can you build?

A young man told me about a girl he used to date. She was a beautiful creature. Her face looked like a rare pearl and General Motors could never have assembled a body like hers.

When they went places people looked in their direction. He enjoyed the attention. The young man imagined many others envied him and he was probably correct. He thought about that figure more than he really needed to.

Suddenly the facts woke him up. He found she had the personality of a manila envelope. The only thing they had in common was that both of them liked her shape. This guy was fortunate. He stopped a fancy from becoming permanent furniture.

It happens more easily than we might imagine. Two people have been going together for several months. They have enjoyed continuous physical contact. Thoughts of sex have become overriding in their minds. If they don't find sexual satisfaction, they are certain they will go crazy. They make plans to marry, but in reality cannot see beyond a bed.

For your marital health, ask yourself the question directly. Are you sure this is not a purely physical urge for marriage?

ARE YOU FINANCIALLY ABLE TO MARRY?

There are usually two sides to this question. The first one is: Do you have enough money to get married? The second one is: Do you have too much debt to get married?

Toss the first question around. It doesn't really take money to get married. There may be considerable expense if you want an elaborate ceremony, a new wardrobe, and a honeymoon in Paris. In short, you

119

may *want* more money to get married, but you do not need it.

A marriage license and a minister will cost less than fifty dollars. The doctor's fee can be thrown in. Housing should be no big deal if both are working.

Many couples are waiting until they tuck some money away. If you want to do it that way, you are certainly free. Strictly speaking, it takes almost no money to get married. It may take a considerable amount to do it the way you have in mind.

The second question is vital. Do you have crushing debts which could hurt your marriage?

Enormous debts may affect your marriage several ways. First, they could force you to work too many hours from the beginning. Some partners are working two jobs from the start. This strains a new relationship too much before it has a chance to mature. Marriage is enough of an adjustment without this yoke.

A second difficulty is starting a marriage too poor to breathe. If you start your union with nothing, that is one position from which you can build. When you start it in the hole, the stark sacrifice could become overwhelming.

Maybe you would be far better off to pay those college debts before you get married, especially if they are excessive. It is wiser to work two jobs while you are single than during your first year of marriage.

If you are old enough to marry, you are old enough to count. Possibly your budget can handle your debts. If it can't, solve these needs first.

Many couples are having trouble. They think it is a communication problem. They are having difficulty in their sex life. A few are leaning on a bottle. Behind some of these conflicts there is a financial pressure which is causing the other difficulties. Their debts are like a swollen thumb making the entire body miserable.

"Just as the rich rule the poor, so the borrower is servant to the lender" (Prov. 22:7).

ARE YOU A RUBBER DUCK?

When we were children we had a yellow rubber duck. We liked to play with it in the tub. You could hold that duck under the water for a long time. Every time you let go of it the duck always bounced up again.

Ask yourself what kind of rubber duck you make. How well do you bounce back?

Some days marriage hits the floor like a rock. You lose sight of your hopes and dreams. You become discouraged and think this thing is a disaster.

At this point your ability to bounce back may be your saving factor.

One evening your partner slams the door while stomping out of the house. You have harsh words and he leaves in a storm. While he walks around the neighborhood to cool off, what is going through your mind? You are down. Probably you are disgusted. The big question is, can you bounce back?

Will this or something like it be too much for you? Will you take it so hard you can't bring yourself to heal it?

Your marriage is going to have some bad days. How bad they become may depend on your ability to get off the bottom and surface again.

The most beautiful word in the English language is resilience. This is what a rubber band does when you stretch it. The band snaps back into shape.

Your marriage can break down. It is much like everyone else's. When it does, tell yourself, "We will be back in each other's arms. We are a couple of rubber ducks."

God is the father of sincere hope. Even when things are down, he reminds us of what will live again.

"So I pray for you Gentiles that God who gives you hope will keep you happy and full of peace as you believe in him. I pray that God will help you overflow with hope in him through the Holy Spirit's power within you" (Rom. 15:13).

CAN YOU ACCEPT RESPONSIBILITY?

It was fun being single. During college I lived at home, and at my age my parents asked little of me. I had dodged the school dormitory, so I wasn't under supervision. Most of the time I did what I wanted.

Marriage changed that. Not harshly or painfully. The fact was, I was no longer free. I had volunteered to restrict my activities. Could I live happily with this new responsibility?

Responsibility is not an ugly word like shackles. It is a wholesome word like maturity. Are you mature enough to accept the healthy responsibilities of marriage?

You will have a responsibility of time. Now it will matter when you come and go. That is good, because it proves somebody cares.

There are new meanings to the clock. Dinner time isn't just a matter of cold potatoes or lost money. Now it is a question of being on time because someone you love is waiting. They went to a great deal of trouble to prepare a meal for you.

Bedtime means something else too. You don't stay out till 1 A.M. without calling. Someone is waiting and counting on sleeping with you. If you aren't there, your partner will worry.

Now you are learning responsibility.

Shared money may be a new adventure for you too. A new husband went out to buy a shotgun. His budget wouldn't stand it but he felt he needed it. His wife was stuck with a handful of money which wouldn't stretch far enough.

Money becomes more than self-indulgence. It becomes more than your "right."

A new wife found it frustrating. When she was single she bought clothes as she needed them and could afford them. Now there was a new element in her life. She had to check with a partner to see how far the money could go. She was adding a new dimension to responsibility.

This is one of the reasons why thirty-year-olds have difficulty adjusting to marriage. They have handled their own money and time for a decade. It may be a little harder getting used to sharing.

The independent spirit often has difficulty becoming answerable to anyone. Such a person is used to walking out when he likes. If he plans to go to the races Saturday there is no need to check with his wife. He even considers it demeaning to discuss it.

If you have a potential partner who thinks this way, give marriage a second thought. This attitude is self-centered and immature. Many who marry a partner this irresponsible live to regret it.

Sometimes it isn't important enough to check with your mate. Fine. Leave a note. Tell him where you are and when you will be back. It is the most basic of courtesies.

If you think you are not accountable to your mate, you probably are not mature enough to marry. The same principles apply to performing duties. These duties may not be along traditional lines, but each partner must pull his own load.

A husband in Detroit refused to accept any share in duties. The door was broken but he did nothing. A pipe broke, but his wife had to fix it. They were not switching roles. He accepted no role at all. As far as the home and family were concerned, he practically did not exist.

To become a shadow is to ignore responsibility. You become partners in a marriage—not monarch and slave.

Faithfulness is another basic responsibility. Never settle for being half-married. It becomes a question of total allegiance.

Don't marry someone you can't respect. After you are united, never betray that relationship in any way.

Even in everyday contacts, steer clear of giving the impression you are half-free. By all means, have friends at work or at church who are of the opposite sex. Be cordial and don't be afraid to joke. However, stay away from flirting. It was fun when you were single. It can be misunderstood by everyone after you are married.

A partner should always be able to say, "I know who is number one in my mate's life." Your spouse may doubt your intelligence, your strength, and your sanity, but never cause her to doubt your faithfulness.

ARE YOU USING MARRIAGE AS AN ESCAPE?

Marriage makes a lousy Houdini. You may be tied up in all sorts of chains. If only you get married, you think you will break your chains and fly.

You can't stand living with your parents. Your job is unbearable. College is a bummer and you want to quit. Cooking and housework are driving you crazy.

Are you running away from something? Don't use marriage as a hideout. Are you running toward something? Then marriage is a beautiful isle of somewhere.

After you have settled these questions you will be able to coast into marriage with greater confidence.

This isn't the time to read a chapter on divorce. Yet a couple of guidelines should be mentioned. God did not intend for marriages to dissolve. He feels the same way about it as you do right now. Marriage was designed to be fulfilling, happy, and challenging. When two people become one flesh, they should stay one.

Are there exceptions to this? How does God feel about those who are already divorced? We couldn't begin to settle those questions in a few sentences (however, certainly love and forgiveness are at the center of his attitude).

Some days marriage is no feast. It can seem barren and hard. But remember, divorce is never a picnic. A person says, "I will get rid of these problems and divorce him." Has she considered the new pile of trouble she is about to inherit?

A Marine pilot said he almost bailed out of a plane once. It had been hit by enemy fire and was crippled. He put on his parachute and walked back to the open door. His head peeked out at the thousands of feet of open air and that hard ground. He then turned around, went back, and landed his plane.

Bailing out isn't exactly a cruise to Bermuda. You will be better off trying to land the craft you are on.

Enough of divorce. Your marriage has too many great prospects. Most marriages work and so will yours.

The fact is, you can never go home. With all you have going for you, you will never even have to try.

15

MARRIED SEX IS FUN

What could be more natural than married sex? Relax, enjoy, grow, explore. The marriage bed can be one of the most pleasurable experiences in life. Sex fulfills two basic great needs: to have a good time and to have children. This is the best order, not the other way around.

Let go and simply allow two bodies and minds to enjoy themselves. That is really the primary purpose.

Practically every couple is concerned about how they will act in bed. This is fine and you probably won't completely lose that concern until the first few nights are over. Tell yourself before it begins that in most cases sex works out beautifully. It will also work magnificently for you. Don't let fears, rumors, and strange literature frighten you. The worst enemy of your sex life right now is that you will worry too much about it.

Two young people in love, who do not become unduly frightened, are going to have a happy sex life. You can take that to the bank.

This is especially true when you first get married. You don't have children to distract you. Right now the two of you are probably each other's favorite hobby. Your health is most likely robust and vigorous.

The Bible has an ancient principle which is tremendously practical. Hang it up at some appropriate place in your home.

"A newly married man is not to be drafted into the army nor given any other special responsibilities; for a year he shall be free to be at home, happy with his wife" (Deut. 24:5).

I have a feeling he didn't spend the year just making kitchen cabinets.

But aren't there exceptions to this? Not everyone has an easy adjustment that first year. Correct, and we will discuss some of the difficulties. However, the basic principle remains sound. Most newlywed couples are going to find sex enjoyable, satisfying, and exhilarating. By majoring on the obstacles, we often make married sex a labor rather than a blast.

By speaking too often about the "problems" of sex we may be creating problems. Married sex is fun. Look forward to it as a rich experience and most likely it will be.

To start off with a positive, eager approach, read 1 Corinthians 7:2-5. This passage is cheering on the married couple with unbridled enthusiasm. Nothing sheepish about the Apostle Paul.

He tells the woman to use her body to please her husband. Would he enjoy this or that? Great! Make him happy. This is what married sex is all about.

When you become married your body no longer belongs to you. The bride gives it to her husband: not just for his need, but also for his pleasure.

Before you call Paul a male chauvinist, read further in the text. He tells the husbands that their bodies belong to their wives. No double standard. His body is to be used to please her. Would she like this? Would she like that? He is there to take care of it.

This supposed modern view of sexual equality is an old biblical view. Women were not created to entertain men in the bedroom. Rather, they were made to entertain each other.

Since they fully belong to each other, they cannot withdraw themselves physically without the consent of the other. This applies to both male and female.

Years ago there was an executive who had to be on the road continuously. He could be gone for a month or more at a time. Finally his wife confronted him with the facts. She felt she would have too much difficulty remaining faithful if he continued on the road.

There was no reason for her to feel like a nagging wife for explaining this. She needed the physical pleasure and security. His body belonged to her and she had to have it close. Paul says don't stay away from each other too long. It isn't good for either one of you.

God originated sex—he thought it was a great idea. Sex is not a necessary evil. God is not neutral about sex; he is promoting it. He is saying do it often or you could be sorry.

This doesn't make it the whole of life as some seem to make it. Their every thought, joke, book, conversation centers on one subject. But sex is a terrific part of life and should be practiced freely in marriage.

I told a young couple I had knocked on the door of their trailer on Sunday afternoon but no one answered. He said, "Oh, we heard the knock but decided not to answer it." Then he just smiled. Maybe they were watching Jello chill.

How do you see love? Is it getting or giving? For a full sexual experience, try to look at it as giving. Too often we are looking forward only to getting from sex. This is especially true of men. Sex is something they want, need, and have a right to, rather than something they give. But our sex lives will be even greater if we begin to see it also as giving.

During the first few weeks or months of marriage, sex is often fairly spontaneous for both. There is frequently a healthy fever which keeps the two of you going. After a while it starts to become uneven. He may want more sex than she does. She may want it at different times than he does. They may not want to go about it exactly the same way.

Each partner is wise to become the happy manipulator. It is especially important to give love. The result is twofold. Your mate will become extremely happy and in turn will respond with greater physical love.

When the object of sex is to please your partner, everyone is a winner.

The problem with this approach is that it takes patience and knowledge. Sometimes men aren't outstanding at either one. Many men and some women want instant sex. As one woman put it, "My husband thinks he can swing out of the shower nude on a rope and I am supposed to run to him."

Frankly, this is how many men see sex. And sometimes there is nothing wrong with it. On occasion she may feel exactly the same. But generally this isn't the best approach.

There is no single way to arouse a partner sexually. Each one is different and each may be different according to the time and place. The smart mate will study his partner. Discover what appeals to him and patiently make it work.

As you develop this intimate rapport, talk to each other: "I like that, do this some more." Don't be afraid to ask questions. "Does it feel good when I do this?" Be gentle and generous. If something hurts or is uncomfortable, say so. It is an important growth which will greatly benefit both of you.

One evening a partner may not enjoy something he thoroughly liked the evening before. Say so and add, "But I'd enjoy it another time."

If you can get this far and maintain it, your sex life can only soar. The smart partner studies his mate. "She really liked that; I will do it again."

Generally we assume men are more interested in sex than women are. Don't count on it. We are people and not categories. Women may suffer from two problems: the constant fear of pregnancy and the fact that men have often been lousy lovers. Some authorities believe that a woman's sexual potential may easily match the male's. To discover her potential, she first must stop seeing sex as a duty or a "necessary evil."

In order to make love, a couple has to be willing to experiment. Often a partner doesn't know what turns him on. They haven't tried it so how can they know? Try it. Whatever it is—try it. Maybe you will need to try it more than once before you know what each of you enjoys. In most cases you cannot sit back and guess what you will like. Making love is an art. It is a clay which has to be worked. Thus we gain knowledge of what to do.

But what can you do? What are the limits? What is natural, moral, and decent? To many, sex has meant the traditional missionary position. It, simply stated, is a male having intercourse on top of a prone female. Supposedly it got its name from nationals who knew the missionaries had sex this way. In some dark corridor of history this came to be known as the only "Christian" way to have sex.

Today we not only know better but practice it in a multicolored way. There is no moral sexual position. There is no immoral sexual position. The purpose of married sex is to have fun. How a couple chooses to have fun is entirely up to them. Read that again.

The purpose is to enjoy each other's body. Would you like to touch, fondle, kiss, suck, squeeze, penetrate? This is your decision to make. Can oral sex or daytime sex or twelve climaxes in one evening be wrong? How? Does the Bible condemn these practices? Absolutely not. Just because some people do these outside a marriage context is no reason to reject them. Some crooks wear brown shoes, but that doesn't mean I can't.

There is one absolute law for married sex: close the door.

That doesn't mean you have to do everything. Naturally, you don't hurt each other. Stay away from anything which offends your mate. But anything which both of you would like to try is fair territory. By exploring you might find some pleasures you never expected.

Even in sex we face the temptation of keeping up with the Joneses. We might read a sex manual and find out some couples are doing a particular act. Then we might feel we must do it too or we won't be mature. This is sexual stupidity in reverse. If you want, the two of you can do anything; however, you don't have to do everything.

Again: there is only one absolute law for married sex—close the door.

There are plenty of sex manuals on the market. Some are even specifically Christian in outlook. Generally they can be a help. Correct information has to be better than the old collection of rumors most of us heard. Too many in the previous generation learned about sex only from barnyards or strange writings on walls. Reading dependable sex material is far better.

If you want to buy such a manual (and it is a good plan), be careful what you get. For some engaged couples the books could be more confusing than helpful. A volume of 113 positions can be overwhelming. You would have to be a gymnast to do some of those.

However, after you have been married a while, a manual could prove interesting. After all, there are many enjoyable encounters which we might not have considered.

One of the biggest problems with manuals, films, discussions, or surveys is the pressure to conform. We hear other people are doing this or that and we feel we must do it also.

Don't collapse into this trap. You don't have to participate in every position imaginable. Some are telling themselves, "If that is what everyone else is doing, we should do it also. After all, we are modern and progressive." That little ego trip is not only worthless but dangerous.

As time goes by, learn more about sex. We read about health, foods, temperament, and decoupage. There is also something wholesome in learning about sex and growing. Then do what you think you would like.

It only makes sense to study the subject and study your wife. After ten years of marriage I attended a sex seminar and learned some things about my wife I had never known. When I got home I found out they were absolutely true.

After you have been married a while, buy an extensive sex manual. Every couple of years you might want to read another one. No couple needs to apologize for keeping their sex life fresh.

In all sex manuals, use your Christian guidelines. Group and homosexual sex do not become an open option just because they are discussed in a book.

How often will a couple want to have sex? The national average is around two or three times a week. The problem with this is that some couples will then use this figure as their gauge for success. They think three times is going overboard and one time indicates a maladjustment.

It is another trap. Enjoy sex as often as the two of you like: no more and no less. Then the number will be just right.

In the early days of marriage, sex may be at fever pitch. Later it may have its peaks and valleys. Don't expect a steady line of frequency. After you have been married for several years you might enter a time of increased activity. For months you might enjoy sex like never before. Few things in life continue on an even pace. Sex probably won't either.

Part of what will change the pace is the difference in drives. Husbands and wives are not always ready for sex at the same time or the same rate. Sometimes they are. During the honeymoon and at times during their marriage there might be a close correlation. The rest of the time a great deal of give and take might be necessary.

Two guidelines are necessary in making these adjustments. First, study your mate. Know what turns him on and what turns him off. Only clods will ignore this. Second, remember, the best love is giving.

We have always said it is the wife's job to meet her husband's "needs." The Bible reminds us it is also the husband's job to meet his wife's "needs."

This means there is nothing wrong with merely going through the motions. When your mate is ready and eager, accommodate the person you love. This is true not only of women but of men. A husband can make love to his wife even when he doesn't "feel" like it. Once you begin to "accommodate" you might find yourself more interested than you thought.

There are times when a smart partner will drown his drive. Your mate may be tied up in something terribly important. It might be a good time for you to take a walk, work on your bottle cap collection, or jump into a cold shower. Sex often can wait. A mature, loving couple does not let it rule supreme.

It would be easy to parrot the old cliché about men being more interested in sex than women. I still balk at this. I am not sure it is true.

Traditionally this has been the case. Culturally the sex market is aimed at men. Sexual conquest has been accepted as a sign of great machismo. Maybe we have heard this stereotype until we believe it.

The fact is women have a tremendous capacity for sex. Thoughtful men will appeal to their needs and be all the happier for allowing them to feel free.

Dr. Gale Dunning, a specialist on sexual dysfunction at the University of Nebraska, feels that this is a real possibility. He says "women are potentially superior to men sexually."

Avoid stereotypes. Too many of us believe we have a "role" to live up to. Some wives are far more enthused about sex than their husbands. The opposite can also be true.

For instance, we have often felt the male was more interested in sex because men's sex organs are external while women's are internal. This is *emphatically* not a proper conclusion. Go into married sex accepting it as it comes and not carrying prejudices into it, like old luggage. Your mate is a person, not a statistic. A part of what kind of lover your partner is depends on what type of lover you make him.

Don't try to be the national average. Don't try to be the woman you saw in a movie. Do what you enjoy and let it flow.

The sexual freedom expressed in Hebrews 13:4 is absolute. "Marriage is honourable in all, and the bed undefiled" (KJV).

Somewhere I heard that Eskimos refer to sexual intercourse as "laughing." "Honey, would you like to laugh a little tonight?" That sounds great. Sex makes a lousy science but a fantastic art. If we worry too much about our "performance" and "duty" we are liable to kill it.

In some literature there has been a great stress on the couple being able to climax together. All over the country partners were working hard in constant fear one would finish before the other. Unable to peak together, they began to wonder about their compatibility.

Don't take it so seriously. If you climax together, that is a lot of fun. If you take turns, that's a real charge too. The important thing is that you remain available while your partner finishes—however he cares to finish.

Many times the partner does not have to climax or have orgasm at all. More often the wife (but sometimes the husband) will enjoy sex for a few minutes with tremendous passion. Women then seem to peak and rescind without orgasm. The partner may feel frustrated as if the mate didn't enjoy it. The fact is, the other was in pure ecstasy. But you can soar with the eagles and still not climax.

I believe other spokesmen have taken some of the joy out of sex by spiritualizing it. I have to bow out at this point. To suggest we pray before having intercourse seems entirely too serious. Is there nothing natural in life? I have to confess I have never prayed before tying my shoes. I have never prayed before selecting a necktie. And I have never prayed before having intercourse. If I did, what would I pray for? Because there are books telling young couples to do this, I have to raise a voice of protest.

If you are engaged and have not yet discussed birth control with a doctor, do it immediately. What form you use should be decided by you and your physician. A safe guideline to keep in mind is to make birth control a woman's device or pill. She is the one who risks pregnancy and she should make sure she is protected.

There are certain sexual attitudes and practices we take into marriage. Our attitudes can improve and refine by education and experience. Some of us will be worried because of our past practices.

One major sex problem in the United States today is masturbation. It affects and bothers more people than any other sex practice. It is estimated that at least 90 percent of single males masturbate occasionally to frequently. Statistics claim 60 percent of the females have performed self-sex. I assume the reader has.

Begin by disregarding every old tale you have heard about masturbation. I have discussed the subject with university students and it is amazing how many believe these myths. There are *no* lasting effects from self-sex. You will not go bald, get pimples, lose brain cells, develop a drool, or go crazy. I have both medical and theological books in my library which insist these are true. One doctor of fifty years ago says, "I can look into a boy's eyes and tell if he abuses himself." Balderdash. It is all nonsense.

Young people who have masturbated frequently will enter marriage with no sexual difficulty or maladjustments. Some problems are blamed on masturbation, but it is not the core of the difficulty. Expect no complications. The few exceptions are too rare to expound.

Somewhere in your marriage the two of you may choose to masturbate each other. It can be tremendously satisfying. For many the practice will simply pass away.

From early adolescence up most of us have participated in a form of lust and mental sexual fantasy. This is probably more the rule than the exception. You can be almost positive this will in no way affect your married sex. Now you have a wholesome avenue to express your frustrated interest in sex.

Often fantasies and lust continue after you have become married. This is frequently true among both men and women. If it is not allowed to go too far, it won't become harmful to either one of you.

After you have been married for a while you might want to discuss your imaginations. In some cases it becomes a good vent for pent up guilt feelings. It may help you understand each other and make you better able to handle stress.

Rather than act as if we never look at another person, it is often better to discuss what and why. Some things do not need to be said. Rude frankness can be ugly. However, open communication can be great.

As your married life routine begins to take shape, make allowances for promoting your sex life. Too many couples become so busy they fall into bed at night too exhausted to make love. Then they wonder what happened to their interest in sex. In fact, it is almost physically impossible.

Make arrangements for lovemaking sessions. Agree that Friday night you will go to bed at 8:00 P.M. for sex. If anyone suggests you go some place tell them you have an appointment. They don't need any more explanation than that.

Plan a weekend away. If necessary plant the children with friends and relatives. Tell them you will do as much for them. Two days alone will go a long way toward getting your head back on straight.

One couple called a baby-sitter and took off for the evening. Just fifty miles away they checked into a motel. All evening they made mad love. At midnight they checked out and went back home. I don't know what the motel manager thought, but we had fun.

Maybe Saturday morning or Sunday afternoon will become a good time for an oasis. The smart partners will carve one out.

Couples often go into a dry spell for a while. Both their interest and participation dwindle to nothing. If this happens, keep your perspective. You are not becoming impotent. Your sex life has not died. Almost all sex difficulties are problems of the mind and the setting. Less than 5 percent of all sex difficulties are physical.

During this lag time, ask yourself what needs to be changed. Is either one of you worrying too much? Are you working too many hours? Is there trouble at the job? Your sex life may be suffering but almost always the real problem is something other than physical.

Practically every bard and psychologist agrees: flesh needs flesh. Experiments with monkeys and humans alike have shown that when all physical affection is withheld, the individual will deteriorate and even die.

Sex is outstanding communication. It says someone loves you. You are important. Someone cares what happens to you. A special person wants to wrap her arms around you, say she loves you and mean it. Someone needs you and isn't afraid to admit it.

No casual sex affair can compare with this. And there are few other things God has given us which can begin to match this type of sharing.

Despite all the information which is available, a few Christians still feel uneasy. They are suspicious that all of this really belongs in the closet where no one can discuss it.

Actually the opposite is true. Sex seems to be exploited all around us and still it is not discussed enough. The amount of misinformation is astounding. The number of unwanted pregnancies is astronomical. The increase in venereal disease is epidemic. We suffer far more from silence than we do from free discussion.

Each of us should read the Song of Solomon frequently. Look at its boldness and candor. The author writes about her beautiful breasts and lovely thighs. Nothing prudish about him. Why did God allow this book to be included in the Bible? Is it because he is far more willing to discuss the subject than many Christians? A definite possibility.

There are several popular myths abroad concerning sex. It is hard to tell who believes them. Sometimes they are propagated in the strangest circles. Mark all the following false.

Myth #1   Sex is a necessary evil.
Myth #2   Women have little interest in sex.
Myth #3   Masturbation causes physical or mental damage.
Myth #4   Oral participation is pagan.
Myth #5   Men are great lovers.

Myth #6   Contraceptives are un-Christian.
Myth #7   Most causes of impotency are physical.
Myth #8   Menopause erases a woman's desire for sex.
Myth #9   Hysterectomy removes ability for sex.

After you have passed this exam go on to the next test. Here are several steps to a happy sex life. Memorize them—your test will come after you are married.

Step #1. Establish a good time. Scores of activities are trying to steal your happy sex time. Decide to fight back or it will suffer.

Step #2. Control your setting.

Make love in some location where you are guaranteed privacy. Trying to love while you are afraid the door will pop open is a bummer. Decide before you start that you won't answer the phone.

One couple was making mad love one night when the shade popped up. Like combat Marines they tried to crawl over and lower it without being seen.

Step #3. Set the atmosphere.

Do you like soft music? Would you enjoy a vase of flowers in the room? Would you like to discuss a sex manual in bed together? It isn't evil to plan your little escapade.

A minister in Michigan had his bedroom decorated in red because it made him and his wife think of a bordello. You might not need to go this far.

Step #4. Sex takes patience.

We don't always want a big episode. Sometimes five minutes is plenty and you go to sleep. At other times early plotting and planning really pays off.

A few suggestions in the kitchen couldn't hurt. A little patting here and there might not be a bad beginning. A good half hour of teasing ahead of time may pay big dividends.

Learn where your partner likes to be touched.

Step #5. Cleanliness.

Both of you get as clean as new sheets. There is no telling what you might want to do.

Step #6. Communicate.

Is there something you would like to do? Let your partner know. You can tell him physically or vocally. He is probably eager to do it, and it sure beats guessing.

Step #7. Explore new ideas.

Let your imagination stretch. You might enjoy it one way for a time and then another. Sex doesn't have to be boring or routine. Try it—you might like it.

One couple decided to love by candlelight. When she tried to pass the candle across the bed she accidentally spilled hot wax on his nude body. It took some of the romance from the evening.

Step #8. Study your mate.

What turns one on may turn another off. Feel free to become physically acquainted.

Step #9. Read a good marriage manual every few years.

The book may not tell you anything you don't already know. However, it might remind you of some things you forgot.

Anyone who has had a satisfying sex life is extremely happy for you. You are about to begin one of life's greatest pleasures.

16
QUICK TIPS

There was a baseball player who could handle hard line drives like an apple picker. He was fast and accurate. The other team started bunting softly toward him. With these easy grounders he looked as uncoordinated as a dislocated octopus.

Don't work on the big questions and flunk the little ones. Here are some quick, everyday tips.

1. Never give up saying "thank you." Familiarity rots a marriage. After a short time it becomes easy to give up on common courtesy. Yet we manage to remain polite to the mailman, waitress, and saleslady. So promise your marriage you will never unplug "please" and "thank you."

2. Be dedicated to a double bed. A movie star was asked how he could stay married for so long while other actors divorced so easily. He said, "It's hard to stay mad when the two of you sleep in a double bed."

Health makes it necessary for some to have twin beds. Anything short of that, stay in a double. I have married friends who say they can't stand sleeping next to someone. Think of what they are missing.

If you have a fight and you want to stay angry you had better sleep on the couch. If you get in bed and start to rub up against flesh you could become friends again in a hurry.

3. Keep secrets. Not the big, important ones but the little "who cares" type. Every person has to have some private life. Don't press to know everything your partner does at work or home. Don't always want to know who was on the phone.

One husband dreaded coming home after work. He knew he faced his daily interrogation. What happened today? Were you busy? When is Stella's baby due? Asking too many questions is pressing too hard. Relax and let your mate tell what he wants.

4. Exaggerate. Tell your wife she looks terrific. Terrific probably isn't the exact word, but marriage isn't a vocabulary quiz.

Many times you don't want your partner to be frank and you might as well admit it. I am learning to ask my wife to exaggerate. I will say, "How do you like the way I painted the cabinet? Lie to me. Say it's nice. I'm too tired to take criticism." My wife then tries to stretch every good thing she can. Next week I'll repaint it.

A husband starts telling his wife how great her dress is. Both of you know you are exaggerating but she still eats it up.

5. Do your partner's duty. Once in awhile give your partner the big surprise. He thinks he will have to rake the front yard when he comes home. What a lift when he finds it done.

The wife gets home after a hard day and finds the dishes clean, the living room picked up, or the hall vacuumed. Little acts just say someone cares. It can really light up a mate's life.

6. Start loving in the kitchen. Don't make loving a time or a place. If you are heading for the bedroom, begin early and start in the kitchen. A pat here and a stroke there. By the time you get through four rooms in the house you will both be ready.

7. Allow plenty of private time. I love Friday night basketball games. Once a week my family goes to the game and I stay home alone. The living room is all mine. If there is something good on television I can watch it without moans or groans. I read the newspaper, a couple magazines. Basketball is becoming my favorite absentee sport.

It is easy to smother your partner. Some spouses even feel it is a sure sign you are in love. Smart partners give enough breathing room to keep everyone healthy.

Make time when she can go shopping alone. If you have only one car, let her take it to get away. Let her belong to a bowling league without you.

Too much private time is probably a lousy idea. A small dose is a great idea.

8. Do something once a week you don't like. Put her record on even if you think it sounds like broken dishes. Play a game she likes even if it is Tiddly Winks. Don't wait to be asked. Suggest it to her just because you know it will make her happy.

9. Be a fair fighter. Sometimes you are going to have words. There are certain ground rules to make it a clean fight.

a. Stay with the problem. Don't bring in other complaints which only cloud the issue.

b. Stay out of the archives. Don't drag up old arguments which keep the wounds open. It is unfair to mention last year's vacation.

c. Stay away from in-laws. If you are upset about the budget, don't use this as an excuse to take a jab at her sister. Keep it within bounds.

d. Stay away from "never" and "always." Some of the world's worst sentences are: "You never help me." "You are always late." "You never say anything kind." "You are always complaining." By stretching the facts too far you make solutions difficult.

e. Never become physical. Don't push. Even nudging can quickly get out of hand.

f. Aim for a conclusion. What can you do about it? How can you improve the situation? Just getting it out in the open is not enough. Let's do something.

g. Never fight late at night. When you are tired you can't think as well. Bring it up tomorrow.

10. Be nice to your partner's friends. It is hard to like everyone but you can be kind. Some of your friends may not be charming. If the person means something special to your spouse, make him feel as welcome as Santa Claus in December.

11. Never kiss her in the ear. The only time my wife ever hit me was when I kissed her in the ear. I was teasing her, and about the third time I kissed her in the ear she pivoted with a deadly blow and rang my bell.

Later she kissed me in the ear and showed me the problem. It sounds like a freight train hitting a brick wall.

There is a thin line between playful teasing and pure aggravation. Learn the difference now. Many of us like to be teased. We enjoy the attention and know our partner cares. None of us likes to be aggravated.

12. Don't do private things in public. It is tasteless for a couple to embarrass friends or visitors. Have you ever seen a couple pawing and nibbling on each other in a store, theater, or park? Mature people control their passions a little better.

The same can be said of arguing. It is fine for a couple to disagree in public. They can take opposite sides of an issue and debate forever. It is another matter to seriously correct each other. Bawling out a spouse in public remains ugly.

13. Stay clean. When you marry, the two of you may have different standards of cleanliness. You can adjust quickly. The best guideline: no one has ever been too clean. Baths and brushed teeth can hardly be overdone.

14. Never flaunt your intelligence. There is nothing wrong with having brains, only with throwing them around. An intelligent and secure person doesn't have to prove it.

If one partner is constantly overwhelming the other, an unhealthy relationship can soon result. Don't make marriage a physics exam.

15. Suggest nice surprises for your partner's parents. It is an extra mile you don't have to go—just something kind and thoughtful. It also shows you approve of the effort your spouse pays toward being nice to parents.

The Bible is packed with quick tips for married couples. Search the Scriptures and find a wealth of practical advice. I'll list just a few.

"A father can give his sons homes and riches, but only the Lord can give them understanding wives" (Prov. 19:14).

"A constant dripping on a rainy day and a cranky woman are much alike! You can no more stop her complaints than you can stop the wind or hold onto anything with oil-slick hands" (Prov. 27:15, 16).

"And you husbands, show the same kind of love to your wives as Christ showed to the church when he died for her" (Eph. 5:25).

"Above all else, guard your affections. For they influence everything else in your life" (Prov. 4:23).

"Better to live in the desert than with a quarrelsome, complaining woman" (Prov. 21:19).

"Drink from your own well, my son—be faithful and true to your wife" (Prov. 5:15).

"A beautiful woman lacking discretion and modesty is like a fine gold ring in a pig's snout" (Prov. 11:22).

"These older women must train the younger women to live quietly, to love their husbands and their children, and to be sensible and clean minded, spending their time in their own homes, being kind and obedient to their husbands, so that the Christian faith can't be spoken against by those who know them" (Titus 2:4, 5).

"A worthy wife is her husband's joy and crown; the other kind corrodes his strength and tears down everything he does" (Prov. 12:4).

"It is better to eat soup with someone you love than steak with someone you hate" (Prov. 15:17).

"Love forgets mistakes; nagging about them parts the best of friends" (Prov. 17:9).

WEDDINGS AND HONEYMOONS

The purpose of a wedding is to get married. The second purpose is a social function. Don't get these two confused. Plan a wedding you can enjoy.

To keep your wedding where you want it, remind yourself of several guidelines.

Plan the wedding you want. Don't give in to the pressure of keeping up with the Joneses. If you want a forty-pound cake and tons of flowers, by all means have them. But if you want to get married in a living room with a collection of eight relatives, please do that.

Let a wedding be an expression of your personalities. Make it a fulfillment of your dreams. When it is allowed to become a forced exercise, a wedding can easily become a tension-filled hassle.

In our culture a wedding is usually the bride's domain. Often her parents pay for the ceremony, or she does alone, or the new partners pay together. In any case, she normally decides what she would like. Because they love each other, the partners will come to reasonable agreement as to what suits them both.

A word to the new husband—go along. Most women have been dreaming about their wedding for years. Whether they want it simple or ornate, they often have the mental picture set in stone. Let it be her wedding. In many cases all the groom has to do is show up. If he keeps saying yes through the entire service, he will end up married.

She needs to be sensitive to your personality. If it might give you a stroke to memorize your vows, then let her know. Reciting a poem may not be something you can handle.

If she has a set dream, try your best not to upset it. There is nothing as lovely as a happy bride.

Hopefully her parents will also give her good support. In most cases they go as far as they can. Sometimes parents are determined to make this their marriage. A few feel that if they are paying for it, they call the shots. That's too bad. It can then become a social occasion aimed primarily at pleasing the parents and their friends.

I married a couple who wanted a simple wedding. They wanted a few friends in the church, no reception, and they would leave immediately for a camping trip. This was their life style. They were a jeans couple and wanted to stay that way. Soon their parents were taking over and making it a ceremony neither of them wanted.

Most parents are extremely helpful and understanding. If yours are that way, kiss them twice a day.

Whatever your plans, keep them within your grasp. Some brides are making dresses and rewriting music at the last moment and their weddings become nightmares. A few weddings become too much of a headache. More than once feelings become strained and arguments erupt. Don't stretch your plans beyond what you can comfortably manage.

Our present wedding practices are not eternal. We didn't always do it this way. It isn't pagan to change the music. Many of my old friends in the Midwest were not married in churches. In those days it didn't seem necessary or proper to have a wedding outside a home.

God's blessing isn't restricted to church weddings. He doesn't confuse the wedding and the social function. The wedding of a good looking couple named Isaac and Rebekah is recorded in the Old Testament. In that case the marriage ceremony was simple. He took her to his tent (Gen. 24:67).

The color dress the bride wears is not dictated by God either. If you want to wear a white dress, by all means do it. Your clothing doesn't have to be a commentary on your virtue. That would be cruel.

Alternatives to the traditional ceremony are real possibilities, and most clergymen will go along. You may not want an underwater ceremony in scuba suits as one couple had. Your first choice will probably not be on roller skates, even if you want to get off to a rolling start.

Would you enjoy a wedding in a garden? Would you like it as part of the morning worship service? How about in a living room? In a judge's chambers? What is your dream? Feel free to try to make it a reality.

Whatever your plans, a few people should be told immediately. Let your parents know what you have in mind. When we say the word wedding, we may be picturing completely opposite scenes. They may need time to absorb our idea.

As soon as possible, notify the minister (or judge). Don't assume he will be available. Clear the date and reserve the building if necessary. Lay out your plan and let the minister know just what you have outlined. Don't assume he will do it your way or read your prayer until you ask him.

Most ministers have a pet peeve. (I don't like flash cameras and amateur photographers after the processional.) Ask if there are any practices he would rather you didn't do. Ministers aren't bashful.

To take a minister for granted is both rude and unwise.

Do you want a second minister to help with the service? This is often done, but again the resident pastor should be contacted early. It is a little like planning a party at someone's house without telling him.

A very few couples want to elope and tell their parents later. Think that over at least twice before you do it. Some parents wouldn't care—they might even enjoy it. But most probably would feel hurt. Don't start off your marriage with relatives confused and crushed.

If you are concerned about the predominant etiquette, buy a book on the subject. The most important guideline is to be polite and considerate.

However your plans develop, avoid financial distress. Don't hope for your parents to pay for a wedding they can't afford. You have to evaluate the situation by communicating with them. At the same time, do not hurt yourself financially. A newlywed couple doesn't need a thousand- or two-thousand-dollar debt for a wedding gift.

Before your plans are firm, check out the prices. Catering, flowers, and photographers may cost more than you expected. If you talk to couples who were married five or ten years ago, the figures are probably far off. The best route is to find out for yourself.

What will happen when the ceremony is over? The smart couple will give careful thought to the honeymoon which follows. Just a few preparations can make it the pleasant dream you hoped for.

Ask yourself some basic questions. Where are you going to go and how far? Don't make vague plans like, "We are going to Kansas City." How far is it? Where will you stay?

Make a reservation for the first night and make it fairly close. After weeks of planning a marriage and a couple of hectic days you don't need a long trip the first day. Thirty minutes to an hour is plenty of traveling time. On the second day you can head for a faraway enchanted oasis.

Imagine yourself tired, emotionally exhausted, and worn out from a three-hour ride. You drive into an area and start looking for a room. "No vacancy" signs glare out like pinball machines. It isn't the best atmosphere in which to start a honeymoon.

How long has it been since you ate? Except for cake, some couples haven't had a bite since breakfast. This only adds to your exhaustion. After you check into your room you might want to freshen up and visit a nearby restaurant. A short pause here is a good investment.

When you come back to the room, you might even want to take a thirty-minute nap. Not everyone needs it, so communicate. Respect for your partner has to be paramount.

Will you begin your sexual pleasure now? Most couples do, but a few don't. More than one bride doesn't wake up until the next morning. Don't be too concerned. Honeymoons, despite their joy, are unpredictable.

Before you begin sex, both partners should take time to get prepared. Bathing seems the most appealing route. She will want to be sure her contraceptive is in order. Maybe she will want to wear a negligee.

Do you want to see each other completely nude the first night? Some do and some don't. Don't force the issue and try not to shock each other.

There is no need for shame. Your lover will love your body. Relax. Enjoy.

There is also no demand to become an exhibitionist. Aim for both good taste and gentleness. As time goes on you will feel freer to express yourself. If you want her to take more off, quietly help her. If she resists, make no commotion but back off. She will get used to the idea as time goes by.

If you have a terrific sense of humor, this would be a good time to keep it down. Trying to shock your new partner is not the route to honeymoon bliss.

One couple checked into an old hotel and started their mating ritual. The nervous young lady went into the bathroom and was soon in the tub. After a few minutes something overhead caught her attention. There was her husband's head stuck through the transom with a smile like a silly alligator.

Their marriage has lasted for twenty years, but the little transom trick isn't the reason.

Another nervy husband told his new bride not to worry about her negligee since he had secretly gotten one for her. She didn't know what else to say but thank you. He said, "Here it is," and opened both his empty hands. The frightened little girl didn't know whether to scream or run. Somehow their marriage worked out, too.

Many funny honeymoon stories will have to go untold. Most were better left undone. Be a lover on your honeymoon; you can be a comedian later.

When the lovemaking begins, what you learned from the sex manual will come in handy. As we said earlier, get one from your doctor. The society talks so much about sex and yet many know so little about it.

Whatever your first sexual experience is like, certain principles apply. Make love, don't just take love. There is a degree of selfishness involved. In most cases if you make love you'll receive back all the pleasure you can handle.

If either or both of you fail to reach full arousal, don't become concerned. Many couples are not able to reach a climax the first night. Most do by the end of the honeymoon, but not all.

An extremely small number become completely disillusioned during the honeymoon and are turned off at the prospect of sex. Sometimes they found it was painful, frustrating, and even dull. The tiny percentage who experience this should not despair. Good sex is worth developing.

Don't grade your sex ability by the first night. It may be bliss or a disappointment. Often the second night is the one you were looking for.

If the first night is particularly awkward, you might just want to stimulate each other with your hands. This has two advantages. First, it is a loving caress until you can get your full sexual intercourse into operation. Second, once you relax and decide to do this, you might find yourself having complete sexual intercourse.

Your first night is at best just an introduction. Even greater pleasure is waiting.

Both individuals should know this might be a painful experience for the female. Her doctor may have made some simple adjustments to reduce this. Either way, be gentle, patient, and understanding.

You are now becoming one flesh. This is the height of Christian marriage. God is pleased. This is not a naughty little necessity. It is a zenith. A rhapsody.

"That the husband and wife are one body is proved by the Scripture which says, 'A man must leave his father and mother when he marries, so that he can be perfectly joined to his wife, and the two shall be one'" (Eph. 5:31).

Whether your honeymoon is a couple of days or a couple of weeks, try to make it relaxing, unhurried, and carefree. Be sure lovemaking and getting acquainted are the main goals. Trying to get to the coast and back in three days is taboo. (If you live only thirty miles from the coast, it sounds like a good idea.)

A little sightseeing is in order, but not much. Under the best of conditions it is tiring to read plaques or climb towers. During the honeymoon it can become maddening.

Don't try to save money by renting a room with kitchen facilities. She can hardly wait to cook, but this isn't the place to start if you want more time together. Usually the fewer distracting responsibilities the better.

But do eat. This may sound strange, but the hours have a way of becoming confused. You probably will sleep in late and it is easy to misplace meals here and there. Before long you are weaker than you thought. Eat regular meals and eat well.

Most couples aren't up to taking anyone along. Forget, "Let's take Mother and show her the Rockies." A few newlyweds feel pressed to take a child with them. Think this one over twice, and then don't.

If your honeymoon is not overly busy and fairly carefree, you will probably look back at it as one of the happiest times in life. One of the great investments of life is to build memories.

A honeymoon can't last forever, but it is an excellent way to get started.

FUTURE FAMILY
–A.D. 2000

Will the family go the way of the dodo bird? Are you about to join an institution which will become extinct? If it doesn't vanish, will it change so much you might not want it anyway?

The family is changing rapidly. Grandmother may not recognize tomorrow's family, but it will be there. Despite the prophets of doom, tomorrow's family may be healthier than yesterday's.

That's hard to imagine, especially if you long for the good old days. Today's generation is different. They have dreams of making an even better world. I can hardly wait to see the life style of my children and grandchildren. Today's youth are sharp. They want families and are willing to work at making them outstanding.

The American family has been stunned. Divorce and other social pressures have struck a terrific blow. However, that blow is often exaggerated. The family is far from down. More people are getting married than ever in our history. Even among those who become divorced, one fact remains: over 80 percent marry again.

Marriage is dangerous. Millions are getting hurt. Marriage is healthy. Many more millions are thoroughly enjoying it.

Our present generation is being rocked by change. Inflation, working women, mobility, urbanization, and television are all affecting us. When these shifts begin to settle, we may end up with stronger families than ever before.

This is more than just wishful thinking. This is hope based on a confidence that God's institution can survive shocks and come out better than ever. I think you share that optimism or you wouldn't be getting married.

Because marriage will be different twenty years from now, it would pay to give it a look. This chapter is no crystal ball. It is an attempt to project. If the present trends continue, what will your marriage and family most probably be like?

This will give you a chance to plan. Do you want to adjust to fit in? Would you rather resist and carve out your own pattern? Either one is an option open to you if you plan ahead and make decisions.

Keep our "ifs" in mind. If the present trends continue, this is the way the American family will function in the year 2000.

The biggest change will be the working wife. When we married seventeen years ago, we could be sure most wives would not work outside the home. When you marry today, you can be sure most wives will.

This is a drastic social change. Our pattern of living has not kept up with this trend. Most women still have the same responsibilities at home as they did before they worked outside. In effect many women are working two jobs. This burden is taking a toll on the family. Female suicides are up. Female abandonment of children is at an all-time high.

If the mother is to continue working, the family will have to shift in some direction. By A.D. 2000 it will.

Men have had to assume roles they previously rejected. Few are accepting housekeeping responsibilities, but more will have to. Households will have to become more efficient. The wife simply cannot continue to do all her past duties.

Because of this trend, I hope both of my daughters will pursue a paying career. Whether they marry or not, they are most likely going to need to work. Today 50 percent of American wives are working and the figures are mushrooming. By 1990 12 million more women will be in the labor force.

Even if they marry a gentleman with a good earning power, they will be better to have a career in reserve. Millions of women later feel forced into the labor market by death, divorce, or inflation. Many of these are completely unprepared to hold a job.

One out of every seven homes is headed by a woman. This figure has doubled during the past eight years. We don't like this prospect, but we can't ignore it.

Some have hoped to put off working at least until their children are in school. Maybe this will fit your program. Often women have difficulty finding a good job if they haven't worked for possibly ten years. Many mothers are not waiting. Almost half of the mothers with children under six are now employed.

The working mother definitely affects the American home. Some Christians believe this trend will wreck it. Maybe you and your partner will map out a plan in which the female will never work outside. Certainly society alone should not dictate our life style.

Don't be too simplistic in blaming the working mother for the family's agonies. The problems are complicated. Studies also indicate many women and families are better off because she works. Cultural changes are difficult.

Some husbands are adjusting well to these patterns and others are not. Accepting housekeeping roles is too much for millions of men.

If both of you expect to work, this is the time to begin discussing roles. Can your concept of marriage handle two working partners?

The roles we play will be different in tomorrow's marriage. Men and women will not be in the exact function they were thirty to fifty years ago. Our ability to accept change will to a large extent determine our happiness.

One unique way to share responsibilities is to split the day. Some couples may want to each work half a day. Suppose you operate a paint store. The husband could work until noon while the wife stays home with the children. During the afternoons she works and he stays home.

Both get to work. Both get to give their children individual attention.

Working has its problems, but it is unrealistic to expect a wife to stay home all day in an apartment.

If the wife's working affects the partner, it also has an impact on children. Tomorrow's children will grow up differently.

In 1960 the average family had 3.7 children. The year 1970 reduced it to 2.5. Presently it is 1.9. Where will it be tomorrow? Now less than 10 percent of the population wants four children or more.

The family in A.D. 2000 will be smaller than we are used to. Birth control, housing, and working wives almost guarantee this.

Where are the children if their mothers work? Day-care centers, baby-sitters, and grandparents are standing in this gap. In recent years the number of day-care centers has doubled. A few are open twenty-four hours a day.

What will the effect be of raising the major part of a generation with limited contact with parents? We can better tell in the year 2000. Some authorities believe it will have a good effect only if two things are controlled. One, if the child can identify with his sitter in a positive way. Two, if parents will make good use of the time they do spend with their children.

Parents must consider the raising of children a high priority in their lives. If clubs, friends, and sports events are first, there is no time to invest in a child's life. The working parent may have time to mold a child if the adult will take it.

A redeeming factor in this work load may result in more leisure time. It is a possibility, but don't depend on it. By 2000 we may be working four days of seven hours each. This may sound remote, but our great-grandparents probably didn't expect the eight hour day either.

If children are to avoid problems during these changes, wise parents will have to make smart moves.

Where will the future family live? Probably in several places. The mobility of the American family began after World War II and has continuously increased. Unless this trend slows, you can almost count on moving.

This year one third of the husbands under thirty-five will move. It has become an accepted practice in business. Some executives consider it essential to fresh ideas and growth. Others are moving just because they are restless.

Possibly with both partners pursuing careers, business may have to slow this down. Some companies are reversing this practice.

Presently mobility is still centered toward urbanization. There is a renewed interest in returning to rural areas, but its impact is exaggerated. There are not enough moves to reverse the flow. The majority of families in 2000 will still live in the urban or suburban areas of a city.

Many urbanites will live in apartments, some out of choice and others out of necessity. The price of homes, the size of families, and the dislike for rose pruning will produce many condominium dwellers.

Not all of these changes will be what society afflicts on us. Often it is simply a question of what we really want. Status, job climbing, envy, and restlessness all play a large part in determining our life style.

Mobility produces its own effects. The family which moves around will have less direct influence from grandparents, uncles, aunts, and cousins. While this may diminish some difficulties, it creates others.

Friendships will be shorter for the entire family in these cases. They will lack deep roots and experiences such as knowing a church body or minister well.

What is the total effect of more frequently changing relationships? What are the benefits? How many drawbacks? To a large extent this may depend on how well the marriage partners and parents smooth the path.

What role will the church play in tomorrow's family? To some extent it will depend on whether the church is looking backward or forward. If its message is, "Let's go back, let's go back," it will lose its touch with reality.

An alert church will try to help the family where it is. The insensitive church will only discuss where it feels the family should be. Can it minister to working mothers and fathers? Will it offer help to the single parent or ignore her? Are there ways to minister to the one-parent child who lacks a mother or father model? Can the church help divorced parents or merely condemn them?

Most churches will help the family of the year 2000. They will do it by offering resources which aid families. They will provide instruction in family living. Counseling will be available for all stages in marriage.

Millions of Americans do not presently attend church. As they find increased help for the family, a growth could follow.

The challenge is there for all Christians. Have some of our teachings about the family been more cultural than biblical? Has our attitude toward the husband as head of the home been overstated? Have we turned him into a tyrant rather than a leader? Has the past attitude toward the working mother been more wishful thinking than scriptural? Has our reluctance to help the divorcee been more an act of ignorance than of compassion?

What are the basic biblical guidelines for marriage and the family? A personal investigation of these will be extremely valuable as we meet future family.

A continuous influx of new and different ideas will flood our families in A.D. 2000. We can never again retreat to the place where we as parents could control the ideas our children sample.

Television will continue to pour information and misinformation rapidly at our families. This isn't all bad. It can even be valuable if it is being matched with information by parents. Our families will be exposed to practically every sordid option in existence. The smart family will make a direct effort to supply solid Christian concepts.